A MONTH
OF DUNKIN'

**ONE MAN'S JOURNEY
FOR COFFEE, DONUTS,
SANDWICHES... AND
STORIES**

ARMAND ROSA

A Month Of Dunkin

One Man's Journey For Coffee, Donuts, Sandwiches... And Stories

Armand Rosamilia

Cover by Jack Wallen

JackWallen.com

Rymfire Books

https://armandrosamilia.com

First Edition October 2021

For The Thirsty, The Hungry… and Those Who Love
Coffee As Much As I Do

Oh, and Shelly. Always Shelly

Author's Note: A Brand New World

When I set out to write this book and drink a lot of coffee and eat a lot of food, it was October 2019. A few months before the world was spun on its head. Maybe I was ignorant, but Covid wasn't a word I knew. Corona was, but only as the beer you put a lime in.

I'd like to think this book was written in simpler times. No masks. No social distancing. You could do whatever your heart desired. Without restriction.

The journey to get this published also took some weird turns, too. A publisher was very interested from the beginning, and all I needed was a first draft and then a contract in return. They went silent in April 2020.

Undaunted, I found another publisher interested, but after nearly a year they decided they were no longer interested in my book. No real reason given.

A third publisher said my book *wasn't relevant anymore* in 2020/2021 and passed on it.

Wasn't relevant anymore? It was a book about a guy who drinks and eats a lot, meets people and talks to them. We needed *more* of this in 2020/2021 and beyond.

I decided I'd had enough rejection for one book, especially one I felt so strongly about. I'd had the book edited previously, and didn't want to touch it again. No thoughts or foreshadowing about what was coming up in the future. No talk of doom or the world shutting down a few months later.

This book was fun to write and hopefully fun to read.

That's it.

Sit back with your favorite cup of Dunkin coffee and a chocolate glazed donut and read. That's it. Lose yourself in my journey.

Maybe someday I'll get out there again in this brave new world and do this again.

Armand Rosamilia
June 23rd 2021

Why Write This Book?

There's a simple answer: I'm a writer.

I am going to tell you I've been blessed a dozen times in this book, and I mean it each time. I'm lucky enough to spend part of each day sitting in a Dunkin Donuts writing and living the dream.

I've written dozens of books and had hundreds of short stories published. I've made enough of a living at this to be able to write full-time. Mostly write whatever I want, too.

Zombies. Ghost stories. Crime thrillers. Nonfiction. Contemporary fiction. Supernatural thrillers. Apocalyptic fiction.

One of my favorite books I wrote was *A View From My Seat: My Baseball Season With The Jumbo Shrimp*, a nonfiction book about baseball. The Jumbo Shrimp are the Double-A minor league affiliate of the Miami Marlins. I got a chance to interview hungry baseball players as well as team staff. The owner of the team. It wasn't just about what happens on the field. The statistics that drive baseball. It was also about the people and their experiences.

And my own personal experiences as a lifelong fan of baseball.

It was always about the people and their stories that drove me. I wanted to find out what makes people tick, what their angle and agenda was, even if they didn't realize they had one, and so much more.

All stories are about the people that populate that world in fiction and nonfiction.

One of the many things I love about my wife is her love of people-watching. Her and I could sit in the corner of a crowded room and eavesdrop on conversations all night. Sometimes we have, too.

I'll make up elaborate stories about them. She'll edit or add to what I'm saying. We'll figure out everyone in the room, and why they're really here. What evil lurks under the surface. What wonderful person is hiding in plain sight.

Their unique stories. Don't we all have a unique story, even when we don't think we do?

The simple goal of this book is going to be talking with normal people from all walks of life, each and every day, in October.

Get something personal out of them. Have them open up and tell me about a part of their life they deem interesting and/or important.

If this was fiction, it would read like a scene from a good book. A touch of the character.

That's the goal, anyway.

This could all go south on the first day, leaving me with no stories and nothing interesting to write about.

People are, after all, people.

Maybe customers and employees will look at me and turn away.

Everyone is trying to get through their day. Some weird guy sitting in the corner staring at them or trying to start a conversation isn't in their plans for the day.

This is really going to be interesting.

My wife asked me why I was doing this book. After all, I have so many fiction deadlines on the horizon. Contracts with publishers and a couple of my own self-published books that are due sooner than later.

A book like this is going to be fun to write, but let's be honest: who will want to read it?

I'm writing this book because I want to. As a creative person, I feel like it's just something I need to get out of me. When an idea sticks in my head I find it maddening to think of anything else until I do something about it, either by starting to write it down as a one or two sentence idea, or as a fully-formed story.

People often think writers come up with an idea and sit down and write it. Then the next idea pops into their head and they move on to it.

I wish.

Right now I have about forty-seven ideas lingering in my mind, all fighting to get out. When I was younger I used to write them down as they hit me, and I filled several notebooks back in the day.

Then I realized, if I tried to write every idea and create a story, I'd get through the first few pages. They might not be good stories. Maybe I am so past this idea it is no longer interesting to me, or another forty-seven ideas are already forming.

My wife gets upset for me when someone will approach me at a book signing and start to tell me about their great idea for a book. I tell them to write it. When they act like I'm crazy for passing on such brilliance, and they're offering it to me to write and then split the millions coming in, I smile.

"I don't need ideas. I have millions of them. I need time," I say. "I need someone who types fast, too. If I could type fast I'd have twice as many books out. Your idea might be amazing. I suggest you write it. I'm good on my end. Thank you."

I don't take offense to it like I used to when I was a younger man. I get it. Everyone thinks writing is easy. String a bunch of words together and you have a book.

If this was as easy as people thought there'd be a heck of a lot more books and writers making a living doing this. Trust me.

Why am I writing this book? Because I have to. Because it's going to consume me if I don't.

Besides that dramatic answer... I love Dunkin.

I run on Dunkin.

My writing is definitely fueled by their coffee.

My goal is not to only talk to people while drinking great coffee, but to learn as much about myself as possible. It's been a few years since I've been out in public writing every day.

Will I be able to do it again?

The next thirty-one days are fast approaching.

The Rules

You gotta have rules. Amiright?

I'll be headed to at least one Dunkin Donuts location each day. Maybe two. Some days maybe even a third.

Unlike in the Northeast, the Dunkin Donuts in Jacksonville Florida and surrounding areas are spread out. Not enough to make it infeasible to go to a bunch, but not as easy as a place like New Jersey or Massachusetts, with a Dunkin on every other corner.

A couple of years ago my wife and I were in New Jersey. I was born and raised there but I've been living in Florida since 2001, so each year we started going up north and spending two or three weeks where I grew up doing a few book signings with a bunch of other authors.

We were in the drive-thru of a Dunkin on a major highway.

She looked across the street and frowned.

I followed her gaze.

"Is that another Dunkin... right across the street?"

I shrugged. "Then you don't have to turn around on the highway. Convenient."

"But… it's right across the street."

When I pointed out the fact the drive-thru at both locations was wrapped around the building, the parking lots were both filled with cars and a steady stream of customers were coming and going, it hit her: Dunkin and coffee is serious business in the Northeast.

While Southerners love their coffee, too, they also love their sweet tea.

I'm not sure what the point was… which you'll quickly realize is going to happen quite a bit in this book. I'm big on stream-of-consciousness thoughts. Hopefully the editor will figure this all out and not pull clumps of hair out while editing my thoughts.

So, besides hitting a different Dunkin each day, there are a few other rules I need to follow.

I won't go back to the same location in October. Each day has to be new places and new experiences. The ultimate goal will be forty or more spots. I think that's reasonable. An extra stop every three days or so. I'm hoping there will be days when I can go to three locations and get some writing in as well as interviews, too.

The other part of this is the food and drink.

I will order something different each time. It might be food and drink. Maybe just a drink. Maybe just food.

But each time it has to be a different item. With so many on the menu and seasonal additions in October I don't think it will be a problem.

I can also cheat a little bit, too: a large hot coffee with cream and sugar is different from a large hot coffee Britney Spears.

Britney Spears? I'll explain it soon.

I don't think it's cheating doing it this way. For me it might even be harder keeping track. Also, and most importantly... this is my book. I literally make the rules.

My personal goal will also be to try new things. I am a creature of habit and usually order the same thing every time and it doesn't matter what time of day it is.

Large coffee Britney Spears (I swear I'll explain it) and a cinnamon raisin bagel with cream cheese.

Dunkin used to carry tuna and I'd get tuna on a cinnamon bagel.

Don't judge me until you've tried it. Delicious.

There are over a dozen sandwiches on the board, and I can mix and match bacon, ham, sausage.

Same with drinks and extras I can add to them, like mocha, French vanilla and pumpkin in October.

I'm not really worried about running out of things to eat and drink. I'm more worried I'll accidentally have the same thing twice, since there are too many options.

Keeping track of what I've already tried might be the hardest part of writing this book and taking this challenge.

I laughed after writing the word *challenge* just now.

As if all challenges could be this delicious.

It's not like I have to train or mentally prepare to eat and drink every day.

I doubt I'll stare at my reflection in the mirror each morning and have to talk myself into getting out there, into the real world, and devouring a donut or three. That doesn't sound hard at all.

I'll also need to use my Dunkin Donuts Perks Card. One of the greatest inventions ever... since bagels and donuts and coffee, maybe. Simply put, my DD Perks gets me some cool things, notably a free beverage after spending so much using the card to buy items. It's like my very own credit card I can only use at Dunkin, which suits me fine. Thank you. There are also some cool deals like buy one get one items or ordering ahead as well as free beverages. Did I mention the free drinks yet?

As for other rules I need to follow? None that I can think of, although I'm sure something else will hit me at some point and I might have to rethink it.

The only way this goes south is if I get caught somewhere and I'm unable to get to a Dunkin one day or a major tragedy hits... although hopefully, even if something does, I can still get to a Dunkin. Knock on wood.

I also have to watch what I'm spending. I'm not made of money, and let's be honest: I'm a writer. We are, by nature, poor. Starving artists and all that jazz.

Actually, I'm blessed to have a supportive wife with an actual career. She supports me in my endeavors, even when it involves her going to an actual job and me going to hang out in a Dunkin each day.

I lead a hard life, but somebody's gotta do it. Amiright?

Tuesday October 1st

1084 Airport Road Suite B, Jacksonville FL at 7pm

Large iced coffee - cream and sugar
cinnamon raisin bagel with cream cheese (last one!)

Triple points, too!

I was ready. Armed with a tablet with external keyboard, a notebook and pen, a stack of the A Month of Dunkin bookmarks and my DD Perks card. No drive-thru, either.

This is the closest location to my house and it's a bit small, with only one table and two seats on a window counter. The traffic flow always seems steady, and by the time the guy in front of me decides on the two dozen donuts he's ordering, choosing each one like life itself depended on it, the line behind me is growing. I always feel pressure if there's a bunch of people behind me. Yes, it makes no sense. Yes, I feel the need to order as quickly as possible, even if no one behind me seems to care. I silently curse the man with the two dozen donuts.

Six people in line behind me so I order and shuffle out of the way. A mom in line is talking to another woman about her daughter at her side, whos maybe six, and taking gymnastics and cheerleading.

The other woman is smiling and starts talking about her daughter, now grown and out of the house.

By the time I get my food and drink and sit at the table, the woman is waiting for her drink and watching me setting up my things. Mom and daughter, loaded up with donuts, have left.

I smile at her and she notices the bookmarks, which I purposely have at the edge of the table.

When I explain what I'm doing, I don't think she gets it, and I wonder if I get it. This was a cool idea in my head, but now out in public and having to put myself out there and actually talk to people, this is frightening.

I'm looking for interesting people with interesting stories, I tell her. Do you have an interesting story?

She shakes her head and starts to walk away.

I'm not sure where it comes from but I get the courage to ask her: tell me about you or your daughter. Anything.

She hesitates and looks around, as if I'm suddenly talking to someone else. When she looks at the bookmarks I realize she thought they were coupons or maybe something free.

I want to hand her a bookmark but then her order is ready and she can't get out of the place quick enough. No glance back. Nothing.

Not that I would've been ready, anyway. I am technologically as primitive as they come, and when the tablet refuses to let me type into my document, I am frazzled.

No matter what I try, it won't let me write. Writing was kinda the reason I'm here to begin with… that and drinking iced coffee and eating a good bagel.

I smile at the next few customers that wander past me, but everyone is there for one thing: their coffee and donuts.

No one is rude, but they're doing their own thing. I can't say I blame them.

I need to be more aggressive, but in a good way, not a used car salesman kinda way.

Even though I worked retail and retail management for over twenty years, I hated every minute of it. I was a really good salesman because I sold myself, not shoes or candy or whatever else I was tasked with trading for money.

But now, sitting at a table, I'm reminded I'm not aggressive. I smile a lot, which starts to hurt my face. I make as much eye contact as possible, but realize I'm not exactly the friendliest looking guy. My look can best be described as a cross between an out of shape biker and an out of shape pro wrestler. Shaved head. Long, straggly graying goatee.

Women do say I have gorgeous blue eyes, although none of them say it tonight.

All of them make fleeting eye contact before rushing away with their spoils.

I resist the urge to pack up and leave.

Maybe I can interest one of the three associates to chat with me, but when I watch them I see they're busy working.

This is not a great start to the book and getting stories from customers and associates alike. My insecurities are firmly kicking me around tonight, and I imagine what would happen if I had a panic attack or...

I'm being dramatic. I know. Maybe I don't need an interview in each location. Maybe I just need a good story... maybe I'm making excuses on day one.

Who knows? This might be a growth thing for me. I hate public speaking. I hate crowds. Despite being a full-time author who's done countless book signings, sat on panels with a hundred people listening to what I had to say, at least at those events I felt in control.

Seated at a table staring at everyone coming in and out is creepy. I'm not sure why I hadn't thought about it. A concept and a book like this was going to take me out of my comfort zone... like, Twilight Zone way out of my zone.

And its International Coffee Day today? I had no idea... but I'll act like I planned this book to start when it was.

A few more looks from customers but nothing more.

I message my wife and tell her I'm bombing. I'm coming home.

She asks for blueberry Munchkins.

I get ten since they're only two bucks, and I know I'll eat at least half of them to drown my sorrows, real or imagined.

Two bookmarks are left on the table on impulse. I'll leave a couple at each stop and maybe customers or employees will grab one and check out the webpage detailing what I'm doing.

Or they'll go in the garbage.

I have no control so far.

Wednesday October 2nd

3270 Emerson Street, Jacksonville FL at 1pm

Large hot coffee, Britney Spears

I used to work as a DJ at a radio station in Flagler Beach in Florida. Friday nights from seven until midnight, working on a couple of different shows. I had a writing show with another author for an hour and then I finished the night with a heavy metal show, playing the music I grew up with. The ride home afterward was awful, though. I was tired and cranky, but I'd stop every week at Dunkin Donuts and get a large coffee, light and sweet.

The guy who worked the overnight in St. Augustine (this is a 24 hour location) started to see my red Dodge Charger pulling up, and he knew my order.

Large Britney Spears, he'd say.

Light and sweet... Britney Spears. It made sense to me, but I never asked him if he said that to every customer or where it had come from.

Every time I order a coffee, light and sweet, I chicken out and don't ask for a Britney Spears.

Weird things you remember.

I'd set up an interview with local Jacksonville noir thriller author Michael Wiley for today at this location. I figured, if nothing else, at least I'd have Michael to chat with.

He arrived on time and grabbed a coffee, sitting across from me.

We talked for the next two hours about writing, and being writers, the publishing business and book signings. Conventions. Social media. Two non-Florida guys from northern climes settling into Jacksonville.

The actual interview (at least the part when I had the recorder running) went about an hour and was delightful. Michael Wiley is charming, intelligent and asked a lot of his own questions.

Quick plug time: you can hear the interview on my Arm Cast Podcast on episode 299. Available wherever you listen to podcasts.

End plug time.

As we talked music played, customers came and went, and I had a great time. I was at ease. I was in control, and this was someone who I not only knew was coming to talk, but had a lot to talk about.

I've been very blessed when it comes to my writing career, but I never take anything for granted. Whenever I found myself getting long-winded, I try my best to shut up and listen to him talk. Why? Because he's been there and done that. He's working with an agent and a great publisher.

Michael Wiley is a guy I could spend hours with, picking his brain. He's in a place I'd like to be when it comes to crime thrillers. This is a guy I can learn a lot from.

I just need to be cool. Don't get pushy. Don't get weird.

He leaves smiling, so I imagine I didn't get weird with him. Or, if I did, he's too much a gentleman to say anything. I guess I'll find out if I ever get the nerve in the future to message and see if he wants to go to lunch or dinner so I can pick more of his brain.

I leave Dunkin happy I got at least one good chat in, even if it was actually for my podcast.

It still counts to me.

Now I need to talk with an actual customer and get a story from them.

I'm off to a second location. My goal to do more than the thirty-one minimum stops is heading in the right direction.

3929 Hendricks Avenue, Jacksonville FL at 4pm

Large Ice ChocAuLait
2 chocolate glazed donuts

Despite the large and inviting inside of this location, they seem to do big drive thru business. I sat down and I was alone except for the employees. Associates. Workers. I'm not sure what they actually call themselves, although by name would be best.

After nearly an hour sitting and writing, with only a handful of customers coming inside, an older woman comes in and glances at me with a smile. She's staring at the menu, waiting to be served, and she keeps looking back at me.

When I say older, I mean older than me. Maybe sixty. Good-looking woman. She's wearing a too-tight t-shirt and very short gym shorts.

She looks over again and smiles.

Then she gives me a little wave.

I'm confused but I give her a quick half-hearted wave, unsure what's happening.

She's now confused. She wasn't waving at me. At all. She's flirting with her husband in the giant pickup truck right behind me.

I don't know it's a pickup truck or how big he is, and he's a big boy, until she leaves.

But first she actually talks to me. "Oh, sweetie, I was waving at my husband." She's pointing over my head.

I have nothing to say so I just nod and know my face is hot. This is not the way to interact with other people.

After she gets her two coffees, one for her and one for the man who could crush me like a grape, and a dozen donuts, she smiles again at me.

I'd love to say I stopped her and got a great story out of her, but I choked. I nodded at her, made sure not to stare, and let her leave.

I counted to ten and then turned slowly, getting a good look at the big man and the big truck, and he was laughing at something she said.

I had a bad feeling about what she'd told him at my expense.

It wasn't even like I was flirting back with her. I was being nice. I'm happily married. I got carried away because I thought we had a nice icebreaker and I could interview her.

This is not going well for me so far. Unless I invite people I know or want to know, to do interviews, my fear is I'll never talk to strangers.

I go back to work writing my thoughts down as well as work on a fiction book I have a hard deadline for and I'm behind.

At least, if nothing else, I'm out and about and writing while sipping some coffee.

I fight the urge to order a dozen donuts and drown my sorrows in their sugary goodness.

Tomorrow is another day.

Thursday October 3rd

463889 FL-200, Yulee FL at 2pm

Large Signature Latte with Cinnamon Pumpkin Spice

I'm not a pumpkin kinda guy. At all. There are so many combinations to choose from at Dunkin Donuts, but I panicked when I got to the counter and the nice lady smiled at me. As long as I don't get something I've had previously this month I'll be fine.

Cinnamon pumpkin spice tastes like pumpkin pie, which I last had as a small child, when I had no idea I had choices with food. Mom or dad or maybe an aunt put a piece on a plate, put it in front of me with a fork and several napkins, and I took a bite.

Maybe I liked it. Maybe I didn't. I honestly don't remember.

So far, on my whirlwind tour, it's easily my least favorite thing... but it isn't bad. Not at all. I'd have pumpkin again, although if I did it in front of my wife she'd tell me I needed to wear yoga pants while sipping it.

Despite what her opinion is, I bet I'd look fabulous in yoga pants.

I also blame my friend and fellow writer J.C. Walsh, who went insane as soon as Dunkin announced pumpkin everything was back in season.

J.C. could write A Month of Pumpkin book with all the combinations he gets on a daily basis.

And I make fun of him about it on a daily basis. You know what they say about payback…

I've never been a fan of pumpkin things, or Halloween, for that matter.

Not saying I dislike Halloween. I mean, it's just another holiday to me. I'm fifty by the time you read this. Too old to dress up like a very fat vampire or a very fat werewolf. I haven't actually dressed up since junior high, and then it was my Van Halen shirt and way too many bandannas. The mullet was not a costume, unfortunately.

Confession time: despite making my money the last seven years as a full-time author writing horror books, I'm not a fan of horror movies. Haven't been since I was a teenager. There, I said it.

I can't tell you how many times I've been interviewed and the interviewer will ask me about horror movies and I have to admit I'd rather watch a Jennifer Aniston rom-com than the latest remake of a classic horror film.

Growing up, my mother's big holiday was Halloween. She'd get dressed up in wedding gowns she found at the thrift store and apply a generous amount of blood and creepy to it. Then she'd gather up her friends and they'd head to the diner for lunch.

I get my love of horror fiction from her but not her love of Halloween.

Why am I even thinking about this?

Cinnamon spice and pumpkin.

And J.C. Walsh.

I'm wondering if he'll even read this when a small miracle happens: a woman reading a Bear Grylls book nods at me.

First, I had no idea Mister Grylls wrote books. I thought he hung out on mountains and made fire out of rubbing two blades of grass together.

Second, she sits a table away from me despite a few empty tables.

This location has a few spots to sit and seems to be relatively new based on the work going on in the parking lot. I've never been here but I've driven past a few times over the years and I'm not sure this set of buildings existed.

Back to the woman reading the book.

We're making eye contact and not, I hope, in a creepy way. She seems interested in what I'm writing and the bookmarks on the table.

I lift a bookmark up and ask if she wants one.

"You can never have enough bookmarks," she says, and the ice is broken. Shattered. Cracked.

I ask how the book is and she tells me it's good so far. Then I slip in about the book I'm writing and she is very interested. She's asking a lot of questions about my writing career, where I get my ideas from, how long I've been writing, favorite authors, and on and on.

"I'd love to interview you for the book," I say.

She shakes her head. "I'm nobody."

I disagree. After a minute spent explaining the concept again and why she'd be a perfect fit for the book, she puts my bookmark in her book (replacing the receipt she'd been using) and moves her chair closer to my table as I turn on the recorder.

"What do you do?" I ask.

This question isn't about what job you have. It's all about you as a person.

"I crochet and I knit. Blankets and scarves and whatever else I want to create," she says tentatively. I'm not sure if she's embarrassed or waiting for me to scowl or laugh. Maybe she thinks her story won't be worthy of my book.

It is. All stories are unique and interesting.

"Do you do it for family or to sell?" I ask.

"Both." I can see her relax now, her shoulders not as back. She puts her book down. "It started with my kids. I'd make them throw blankets for their beds. When they went off to college I made sweaters." She laughs. "I think they hated them, but they always made sure to wear them when they came home. Especially since they knew I was going to do their laundry."

She doesn't look all that old but she's talking about her grandkids getting her handmade items, too. "The kids are into all these strange characters from videogames. I had to do a lot of research on The Google to find out what they kept talking about."

She actually says The Google, which I find charming.

Once she'd mastered a few items for them she began to create her own characters and modify what she'd seen out there, and she opened an Etsy shop.

"At my age, I'm selling stuff online," she says and laughs. "It's a few things a week. Nothing really big. I do it because I have so much yarn and other materials in my house. I'm a bit of a hoarder, according to my children. I went to an estate sale two years ago and they had cardboard boxes filled with different colored yarn. Different thicknesses."

She tells me all about yarn colors, consistency and what to look for when buying it, and what the different ones can be used for. I had no idea.

Her passion for it is infectious. I haven't done latch-hook since I was a kid, and I really enjoyed it. My mother would buy me kits to do pillows and small tapestries. I'd spend a few weeks doing it, and I remember being very good and it was so relaxing.

That's what it is to her, too: relaxing.

"I usually come up here or wherever I'm going for lunch and have my bag with me to work if I have something that needs to be finished. Now that it's a job, I feel like I should only do them during the day. At night I read more books."

She sees my glance at her book and she smiles.

"Some days you need to switch it up a bit or it will get stale," she says.

I couldn't agree more. Me out and about each day this month is a definite switching up for me. I'm hoping it teaches me a few things about myself, about other people, and makes writing fresh again.

I'd been in a rut lately. Getting stories written because of deadlines and not only because I wanted to write them.

This book will change all of that… hopefully.

We chat about a few random things for awhile and she takes another bookmark before going back to her book and her coffee.

I go back to wondering how my buddy J.C. Walsh got into my head about pumpkin drinks.

1954 S. 8th Street, Fernandina Beach, FL at 4pm

Ham, egg & cheese on an English Muffin sandwich

I've never been in this location, but it's very nice. The staff is always on the move, and I see a few smiles back behind the counter, too. More people who enjoy their job.

Despite some weird customers, I imagine.

For instance: as I grab my sandwich and dig into it I decide to sit in one of the comfy pink chairs instead of at a table. I have a good view of the drive-thru lane, which is busy.

A woman pulls up after paying for her order. I can hear the employee in the drive-thru asking her to pull up because her order will need to be run out to her car.

Whenever I see this I wonder if they ordered a dozen donuts or a bunch of intricate items.

Back in the day, you had coffee and donuts. Maybe an occasional Munchkin order. I can only imagine how tough it is with all the choices Dunkin offers now, and a lot of them take time to make.

It drives me nuts when someone is too lazy to go inside for more than a couple of donuts, and holds up the line.

I won't start ranting. I swear.

The woman is in her car for maybe thirty seconds. She keeps looking back over her shoulder, at the drive-thru window.

Very antsy.

There are cars behind her, but now I see that she is starting to back up. I'm not sure where she thinks she's going. She is so close to the car in the drive-thru I fear they'll tap bumpers.

The girl working the drive-thru is trying to tell her to move up.

I'm sure the person in the car in the drive-thru is not happy being blocked in, either.

Another employee walks past me to the side door to give her the drink and a bag of food but she's not there.

I get the girl's attention and tell her she's back there.

It's all very confusing.

The Dunkin order is delivered but the woman isn't moving her car, even though the employee walked it out and handed it to her.

"She wants to make sure we put extra napkins in the bag," the employee says with a smile as she comes back in and I ask her what the fuss is… because I'm nosy. I mean, I'm a writer.

The car behind her beeps but she doesn't move up to the door. She's staring ahead as if it's normal to block someone else in over some napkins.

When a handful of napkins are run outside, the woman takes her time sorting everything before leaving.

The guy in the car behind her does not look amused, and I feel bad for the guy. He just wanted his coffee and then get back on the road.

The other fun thing that happens before I leave is eavesdropping on the three older men seated at a table in the middle of the room.

"Did you read that opinion piece in the paper this morning?" one asks. I'll call him Ernie, since that's what the other two guys call him. It makes it easier that way.

Bert says... ok, so I don't know his name but Bert seems fitting on many levels. He gets animated. "I did see it and I immediately had to write him a strongly-worded retort."

Strongly-worded retort needs to make it into a future story I write.

The third gentleman is silent throughout the conversation, a smirk on his face as he sips his coffee.

"I think he took a snip at me in his Thursday column," Ernie says. "Not by name, but he misquoted what I'd written the week before."

Then it dawned on me: these fine gentlemen were reading the newspaper columns and sending off responses and letters to the editor.

In the mail. Not email.

I could picture the three of them, in sync, walking out to their mailbox and putting an envelope with proper postage on it into the box and putting the red flag up on the side of it.

Then they wait for the columnist to read it and perhaps comment in a future print newspaper.

I guess these are weekly gatherings since Bert was already there, waiting for the other two. Each of them brought a newspaper with them as well as printed articles from online.

They dissected each in turn and it became apparent they were solving the world's problems. Politics. City policies. What new businesses were being permitted. Which ones were closing, and their take on why.

"I still have that property in Laurence Harbor," Ernie said. "My son thinks it's worth something but he's not getting his hands on it. Sad I never built on it."

I perk up at this. When Ernie glances at me I nod. He nodes back.

"Laurence Harbor in New Jersey?" I ask. I can't help myself. I don't want to be sucked into their conversation but I'm a New Jersey guy. It's what we do.

Ernie smiles. "You know it?"

"I know it well. I spent a lot of time in Old Bridge and that area. Matawan and Keyport," I say. "I was born in Newark and grew up in Belford, part of Middletown."

Side note: I love telling people I was born in Newark. Most people will nod sagely, knowing it is a tough city to grow up in. It's impressive to tell people.

Of course, I moved down to Belford, a small fishing village not known for big city problems, when I was about four.

I chat with Ernie for a few minutes about the food we miss, the traffic and snow we don't miss, and he brings up the Yankees and Mets.

Instead of telling him I'm a Red Sox fan I smile and nod along, knowing the trio will pounce if I go against their opinion, which right now includes the Yankees winning the World Series.

I really hope they don't because I dislike the Yankees more than any team in baseball... because Red Sox.

Maybe when this book comes out they'll all read it and immediately fire off a written letter to my publisher about their precious Yankees.

Great side note: the Yankees didn't make it to the World Series. I am happy.

Friday October 4th

842 Dunn Avenue, Jacksonville FL at 11-ish am

Big N Toasted sandwich with bacon
Large cold brew with cream and sugar

Technically, I was here on-time… but I went into the drive-thru like I've done a hundred times before and then felt like an idiot when I started to order. I apologized and drove around to the front and went inside, hoping no one would notice. If they did notice, they were nice enough not to laugh and point at me.

The gentleman ordering in front of me was a big dude. Like… Marcell Wallace from *Pulp Fiction* big. He had an Egyptian symbol tattooed on the back of his shaved head. He looked menacing and mean, and I'm sure his likeness will appear in a future book.

He ordered something with weird ingredients.

I didn't snicker or laugh or ask if he was picking it up for his wife.

Not cool, and I like me teeth.

Once I sat down in the corner I set up my stuff.

Let me backtrack for a second, though: I sat in my second choice of seats. A woman was spread out in my first choice of seating, which was in the corner overlooking the room. From there I could have a chance to talk to people after they grabbed their order but before they were out the door.

I stare daggers at her and her laptop but she doesn't even look up at me. If she did look up, I know I would've looked away, anyway.

The Big N Toasted was very big and... very tasty. I'd get it again. Filling, even.

Two other things happened while I was writing and trying not to mind my own business: a haggard man wearing dirty clothes and an old Atlanta Braves baseball cap came in. He looked distraught.

When he turned and saw me, near the door, he tried and failed to smile. "Sir, would it be possible to call this number for me? It's my boss and I'm really, really late for work. Four hours late. It's a local number. Please help me."

He handed me the number and I called and handed him the phone.

Let's be honest... I'm suspicious of anyone wanting to talk to me, and if they ask for a favor, it's usually an angle. Sure, it might be an angle I write into a book, but I don't want to get ripped off to learn it for a story.

I hesitated. I admit it. Was he going to dash out the door with my phone? Was he going to call someone he wasn't supposed to call, and now they'd have my number? Right now the FBI was listening in, sitting in an unmarked van and pulling up my information.

Hmm. I smell a book idea.

The FBI (as far as I know) wasn't listening in and I felt bad for the guy because he was groveling to his boss, begging him to pick him up so he could earn some cash today. 'I'll work late. I'll work the weekend. Whatever you need. I've never been this late before.'

After more begging and the guy apologizing to me for using my phone, he sighed in obvious relief. 'He's coming to get me.'

I asked if we could chat for a few minutes while he was waiting, and explained my project.

'Sure.' He sat down across from me and shrugged. 'What do you want to know?'

I wanted to know about him.

'I'm a local.' He grinned, showing me a perfect set of teeth. 'Lately I'm really local, living in the woods nearby. Bad luck. Dumb luck. Poor choices in friends and women.' Another smile. 'Ain't that the answer to everything when you think about it? It's all about poor choices. I have a college degree. Engineering. Come from a good family. If I told you my name, my last name, you'd know it after spending any time in Jacksonville. They're all gone now. Accidents, disease, old age. I'm the last and I'm not living up to the family name.'

I asked if the name, whatever it was, created undue pressure for him. I was expecting a string of excuses.

"Nah. I made the bed I'm lying in, and it's usually a patch of grass under the stars. I can't even blame it on drinking or drugs, either. Just always doing the wrong thing." He's still smiling. "I do make my own rules, though. There is that. Freedom isn't overrated. It's a great motivator. Now I just need to get my act together. Save up some money. When I was a kid we vacationed in Ireland. You ever been?"

I shake my head.

"Really nice. I guess I have family there still. No idea. Haven't been back since I was in my teens. If I could live anywhere it would be there." He's looking off and I imagine he's there right now, living the great life he had as a teenager.

He slaps the table, jarring my tablet and recorder. He extends a hand and stands. "Thanks for the conversation, buddy. I see my boss pulling in. I hope the book sells millions and you get to see Ireland or wherever you want to visit."

"Good luck to you," I say, and I hope he finds what he's looking for. I really do.

I'm blessed. I'm able to not only live my dream of writing, but the mistakes I've made in my life (and we all make mistakes) haven't crippled me yet. They've been learning experiences. Being human.

I'm sure there is more to his story than he's told me.

I'm sure there will be more to everyone's story than they tell me.

People love to talk about themselves, but they give their version of reality. Subconsciously what they want their story to be. Everyone is the lead in the play, to use a tired metaphor. No one wants to be a bit player. They want the spotlight on them for the big song and dance routine at the end. They want to be the hero of their own play.

Maybe he'll get past his past.

Maybe I'll see him in this Dunkin in the future and he'll give me a nod and a smile, and he won't look distracted and worried about losing another job.

I pack up and head back to my great life.

Saturday October 5th

11857 San Jose Boulevard, Jacksonville FL at 10am

Medium hot coffee Britney Spears

Fire Roasted Veggie Bowl - Double points, too!

"Crazy how the kids today can work those things and guys like us struggle with the simplest part of it."

I look up from my Burrito Bowl to see a smiling older man pointing at my tablet.

"I'm still fighting this thing, trying to get my sausage fingers to not hit three letters at once," I say. I wish I was trying to be funny. After less than a week of using the tablet I'm making more mistakes than typing actual words.

He's an older man with a big smile. I return his smile and ask him if he has time to chat with me. He seems excited and joins me. When I explain what my project is he smiles even wider.

"I'm Larry. Pleased to meet you." We shake hands and I turn on the recorder. This seems too easy. He literally came to my table and started a conversation, which is what I was hoping would happen during the month.

I ask him where he's from since no one is born in Florida.

"I was born here in Jacksonville. 1948. I'm the only one, I think." he laughs. "A lot of people are from somewhere else, which is fine. We're a military town. Always have a lot of different people in and out of Jacksonville. It's a good city."

I ask him to describe himself in one word and he doesn't hesitate. "Jesus. I'm seventy-one years old and a born again Christian. It changed my life when I was thirty years old."

Larry is one of those people who makes you relax. Calm. His smile is infectious. I know if I wanted to, I could sit and talk about anything and everything with him until Dunkin closes tonight.

I ask why he's hanging out in Dunkin today.

Larry smiles. "For this. Having a conversation with another person and asking them if they believe. I came here because I like this place. I get coffee and something to eat. I sometimes make conversation with people. It just happens. I get up in the morning and decide to come over on my bike. It's a long ride and I enjoy it. The ride is good for my mind and my heart. I like their coffee better than any other coffee. I drink a cup of Dunkin at home and then a second when I get here. I'm a big fan of the pumpkin spice right now. Great time of year."

We talk about the gallons of coffee I drink every week. Heck, every day sometimes. I'm hooked and I love every drop. I ask Larry if it's hard to start a conversation with someone to chat and find an icebreaker to engage.

"It's always a challenge to approach someone in a public setting because you never know how they're going to react." Larry shrugs. "It's worth giving it a try, though. Sometimes nothing happens. A simple smile and greeting and then it's over. I still find value in it because you've had an honest connection to them. Maybe they'll carry that with them the rest of the day or pay it forward."

I ask if he's always been like this, eager and willing to chat with a stranger.

"When I was a kid my daddy would take me to a restaurant and everybody knew everybody. If you didn't know the person walking through the door you said hi and just started talking to them." Larry smiles. "I started doing that here."

Has Larry ever had a really emotional conversation with someone in Dunkin?

He nods and there's the smile again. I can tell there have been quite a few.

"I had a conversation with a guy just the other day. I could tell there was turmoil on his face. I made eye contact and asked him how he was doing today. He seemed puzzled I was saying anything to him. I told him my generation always talked to people. He said his generation texts one another. Not even close to being the same thing. I asked if he wanted to talk and he said yes. It ended up being such a pleasant conversation. I asked him what was bothering him. He said his wife only cared about money. She was a recovering alcoholic. He was having a hard time in his marriage and was sitting there thinking about ending it. I told him to really think about it. Not to jump to anything. They have children. Go home and love your children. We talked some more and then he surprised me. He looked me right in the eyes and smiled and said he realized he was the only one who could help her. I told him to pray. Give himself to helping his wife and see it through. Whether or not it works out is up to the both of you, but you won't know until you try. Give it everything you have. See it through. In the future you'll feel good that you did whatever you could to make it work, and your children will know you did, too. You'll have a clear conscience knowing you gave it everything you had."

How often is he making the trip on his bike for great coffee and conversation?

"I come here about three times a week. I don't always find someone to talk to. That's just the way it works out. But every now and then you strike up a great conversation. I found people like to talk. Everybody has a story to tell and they like to tell it. Someone has to make that first connect. The smile. The eye contact. Whatever."

Even a small back and forth might mean something.

"I made a comment to an older man the other day about his shoes. He has the same pair that I wear. That sets me up to have something to talk to him about. Maybe not in that moment but in the future when I see him again. I believe we live in a lonely world and a lot of people just want to have an honest connection with another human being."

Larry is trying to make his little part of the world a better place. He should be writing a book about sitting in a Dunkin interviewing people.

When the conversation is winding down I feel great. His positivity and beliefs are touching me, and I know the rest of the day will be amazing.

Anyone Larry is able to touch will have an amazing day.

"It was a pleasure meeting you and good luck with the book. Amen." Larry shakes me hand and is out the door with a smile.

Sunday October 6th

2274 State Road 16, St. Augustine, FL at 11:30am

Large Signature Latte hot cocoa mocha
Chicken bacon croissant

This location was packed. Close to noon on a Sunday, which makes sense. I was going to order something and ask for it Britney Spears, but I chickened out and ordered a chicken sandwich instead. See what I did there?

There are plenty of seats in this location but most were taken. There was only one big table, occupied by a single person.

Side note rant: young people. The woman was probably in her early twenties, and she was at the table. With an empty coffee cup in front of her. On the big table that could seat four. Playing on her phone and ignoring everything going on around her.

Be aware of everyone else in the busy store and move. There were people with kids who were pulling tables together to let the entire family sit, but all she had to do was look up and be a nice person.

I was lucky when I got my food and drink and a table opened up with one chair. As soon as it began to clear out, the rush gone, I was able to move to the counter space.

The entire time I was here writing, observing and chatting, the young woman remained at the big table grinning at memes or funny videos or whatever young people found amusing.

Done with this rant but I'm sure there will be plenty more by the time this book is done.

I find dealing with people is a chore for me, and I don't like feeling that way. I'll be fifty this year, which I probably mentioned already. Feel free to send me well-wishes and gifts on or around November 21st each year.

The older I get the more I want to stay inside and write and stay in my safe little world.

If I'm being honest, today was a hassle to get up out of bed and get dressed and leave the house. Not sure why. It's a gorgeous Florida day, low 80's and a great breeze. I drove with the windows down blasting 80's hard rock tunes and singing along.

Once I'm out of the house I'm fine, but it's like pulling teeth to get me going.

If nothing else, this book will be about finding a nice balance between hermit and social butterfly.

Instead of writing I listen in on random conversations. Kids telling parents about their day. The group of young girls arguing over which donuts to buy for their dozen. I want to tell them to each pick two and since there are five of you, I'll do you a favor and take the last two donuts. My goal is to help them, I assure you.

This is also the location where I found out about ordering a coffee Britney Spears.

Since it's a gorgeous Sunday at lunchtime, families are coming and going like mad. Moms in yoga pants. Dads in khaki shorts. Kids in their play clothes. All chatting excitedly about which donut to add to their box of a dozen.

I'm seeing lots of dozens of donuts going out the door. I wonder how many donuts get purchased each day at this location, and what the yearly total is.

Not enough to actually do any research, mind you. Just wondering.

I was supposed to meet another local author, a woman I'd never met in person, but we got our lines crossed and I came to the wrong Dunkin.

Now I'm worried that no one will talk to me despite the inside being packed with people. Most of them are with someone else, and they seem locked into private conversations as they drink their coffee and eat their muffins.

At the counter I'm seated in the corner with a couple of chairs next to me, but so far most people are using the space to set their items while they get napkins and a straw before leaving.

Finally, two young guys wearing khaki shorts and nearly-matching striped shirts have a seat.

I don't say a word but I'm typing and one of them is glancing over to see what I'm typing.

Hey, total stranger. How's your day going?

I literally type that and he laughs and whispers to his friend.

Emboldened, I look right at them and explain what I'm doing.

"How cool is that," the first guy, John, says and laughs. "I wish I read more."

"I never read anymore. Not since high school," his friend James says.

I tell him it pains me as a writer to hear they don't read for pleasure or to gain knowledge. Even to kill time in the dentist's office.

They're on their way to Gainesville to see their girlfriends. Spend the day hanging out and going to dinner with the ladies before heading back to St. Augustine and work in the morning.

"My girlfriend started college this year at the University of Florida," John says. "We dated all through high school. I didn't want to go to college, though. I work for my dad in his garage fixing cars." He shows me his real working-man hands. Grease under his nails he'll never get rid of. Calluses and scratches on his hardened skin.

My hands are so soft and fleshy from not using them to do anything but type and carry candy it's ridiculous.

"I work there, too," James says. When I ask him if that's where they met he shakes his head. "We grew up in St. Augustine together. Since third grade."

John smiles. "When I helped my girlfriend getting her stuff to her apartment in Gainesville, James went with me. That's where he met her roommate."

James was grinning, too. "She's awesome."

So they're dating the roommates?

They're both nodding and looking quite happy.

"We run up every weekend to see them," James said.

I chat about the area and the fact I had my first date with my wife in St. Augustine and I proposed to her here as well. It's a special city for us, and we love coming back every now and then and enjoying the food, the shops and people-watching.

When James goes to the bathroom I say, as a joke: so what happens when the roommate isn't into your friend anymore? Does it get awkward?

It is just something goofy to say. A total joke. That's my sense of humor.

John glances in his friend's direction to make sure he's not coming back.

"My girl says she's really not totally into him. I mean… she likes him. He's a really cool guy. My best friend. But I think she has a guy back home and…" John shrugs his shoulders. "I guess we'll see what happens." He frowns. "Is this going in your book?"

"I hope so," I say with a grin. "Unless you don't want me to add this part. Seriously. It's no big deal."

He seems to ponder it for awhile silently until his friend comes back.

They clean up their empty wrappers and take their coffee with them. I thank them both for the time and the interview.

John leans over and gives me a nod. "You can use it. I have a feeling, by the time the book comes out, it will be settled anyway."

The two young men both shake my hand and wish me luck.

I make sure to give them two bookmarks each, even though neither of them will use the bookmarks to hold their place in a good book.

The chicken bacon croissant, by the way, is delightful. I'm glad I ordered it, thinking I'd scratch it off my list and not have to eat another one again.

Wrong. I will definitely be eating them in the future.

I also hope to find out what happens to James and the roommate when this comes out, too.

Monday October 7th

10379 Atlantic Boulevard, Jacksonville FL at 11am

Large iced macchiato - Free!

I used one of my free drinks via my DD Perks card. I hoard these free drinks like mad and I don't know why. I always want at least one on standby in case I'm lost in a foreign city without my wallet or cash, only carrying my cracked phone after fighting off a gang of hoodlums. Maybe a sewer alligator. I'm dying of thirst. If the gator couldn't kill me, maybe the thirst will... until I cash in my free drink and grab a large iced macchiato.

See? It makes sense now.

The only time I've ever messed up and lost one was during the hurricane that recently passed through the area. Actually, it didn't even hit us. Not even a quick rainstorm. But the Dunkin locations in the area closed early each day, which made sense. People need to be safe.

I was too lazy to leave the house during the day, supposedly preparing for the storm but really watching a lot of Netflix in case the power went out. You don't want to watch half a season of *Fuller House* and not know what happens next.

So, it was definitely my fault for not cashing it in. All that hard work down the drain. All those delicious coffees and sandwiches and donuts I ate just to get a free drink.

My wife thinks I'm either crazy or goofy (depending on the day) when it comes to my obsession with racking up points for another free beverage. I know I have a month to use it or lose it, and I will check it every day to make sure I'm not messing up.

I was about to say every few days, but that's a lie. Every single day without exception.

The Dunkin Donuts Perks app is on my phone. I check it on my computer as well. As if it's any different.

As I'm writing this I take a break to double-check, even though I know I have until the 23rd to use the next one, and the 27th after that. The last two are for November (1st and 5th) and if I was smart I'd use them this month. I'm sure I'll grab another one or three before the month ends, too.

It's raining pretty hard today. None of the normal Florida rain, where it pours for five minutes and then the sun shines and dries it out in five more minutes. This is clouds and wind and a steady rain, which keeps the drive-thru busy but most people don't want to wander through the rain.

Me included. I really fought the urge to stay home today and maybe wait until it stopped, but I knew, if I didn't go at the posted time I'd never go.

It makes for an interesting time having the place to myself, seated in the corner observing. Today isn't going to be an interview day. I'm too busy listening to the employees singing along to every song playing on the Dunkin Radio.

They talk to the regular customers in the drive-thru, and when a big guy comes into Dunkin to get his order, they all laugh and tell him he's two hours late.

He is making excuses and apologizing, even though they're playing with him. This is obviously a daily routine, and it's cute how they tell him to be on-time tomorrow. He can't stop laughing as he leaves.

I worked retail management for over twenty years, and working with a happy crew makes the day go by quickly and quietly. No drama. No irate customers. No frowning employees who you can tell would rather be somewhere else.

So far every Dunkin I've been in has excellent customer service, and it's one of the reasons I chose to do this book.

Oh, and the coffee, donuts and sandwiches, too.

There's a young girl chatting with the employees and she keeps checking me out, wondering what I'm doing with my tablet typing away. Every time I look up at her she smiles and looks away.

She announces she's leaving and as she starts walking slowly past my table she smiles again.

"How's it going?" I ask... because why not? Maybe we can start a conversation.

"I used to work here," she says, nearly an apology. I guess she thinks I'm wondering why she's hanging around longer than a normal customer. "I just got fired from my other job."

"What happened?"

She shrugs. "Working as a maid at a hotel. They said I was too slow making beds. You believe that?"

I say no, even though I have no idea if she's fast or slow when it came to making a bed.

"Now I'm on my way to catch another job and move on with my life." She grins. "You have a nice day, sir."

And with that she's out the door and into the rain.

I think for a second to ask someone what her name is, but I don't need it. I enjoyed the very brief and very personable interaction we had together. Isn't that what this is about? Snippets of conversations. Seeing a glimpse of someone else.

I don't need a full-blown story about her childhood or every job she's ever worked at. I got enough from her, the important stuff on her mind right here. Right now.

Maybe someday she'll read this book. Maybe she'll never know it exists.

It doesn't really matter.

What matters is her words live on. Her little story. What happened today and how it won't bring her down.

I envy her drive. If that was me I'd roll up and stay in bed all day. Which, when I was her age, I did a few times. This woman just lost her job and means to pay her bills, but she's focused and joking around with her friends.

As she leaves the employees get back to what's important: working the drive-thru and singing all the songs on Dunkin Radio.

I'll be back to this location in the future because it has some real personality.

Tuesday October 8th

*6999 Merrill Road, Suite 1, Jacksonville FL
32277 at 11 am*

Large hot chocolate
Maple bacon sugar sandwich - two times points!

I've stared at the menu every day for over a
week, yet I still find myself stuttering when trying to
decide what to order. I have this weird fear I'll choose
something the night before or maybe right before I
leave my house, and then they'll be out of it for some
reason and throw me off.

Yes, I already know it makes no sense.

This location is in a stripmall and it's smaller
than most of the ones I visit, although it doesn't take
away from the important things like good food and
good service.

With only five small tables in the front, I get
lucky and grab the one in the corner closest to the
door. I'm beginning to feel like Sheldon Cooper in
Big Bang Theory, needing a specific seat.

By the time I finish my sandwich, which tastes
amazingly maple-y, it's raining hard. So hard it's

bouncing off the window behind me and drowning out the music.

Everyone else has cleared out except a guy wearing a blue sleeveless shirt and khaki shorts guarding his coffee like someone is going to steal it.

It'll probably be just the two of us for a while now since most customers will steer into the drive-thru and not get wet. I know I'm not leaving anytime soon.

I wonder how many cars use the drive-thru each day. It has to be hundreds. Right? I'm sure I can Google it and find out but I'd rather be in the dark... and be lazy.

Rain makes me lazy. If I was still home right now, which I normally would be, I'd be on the couch reading a good book until I fell asleep instead of doing any work.

Maybe my wife shouldn't be reading this.

Today I'm working, using the rain background and Dunkin Radio to write some words on a couple of different stories I'm working on.

Just because I'm doing this book doesn't mean the rest of them won't get written. This one just happens to be the fun book.

Let me rephrase that (in case one of my publishers is reading this, or one of my fiction readers): I love everything I write. It's all fun. Living the dream and all that. Being able to create stories pouring out of my head and having people purchase and read them, allowing me to keep writing and publishing my stories.

Sometimes, though, I work on a project for *me*. Like this one. Something I'm not pitching to a publisher or worrying about sales. This book came out of my love for Dunkin Donuts coffee. According to my wife, it's more like an obsession. This is something I thought up a while ago and didn't think too much about it.

Don't worry about anything other than talking to people and getting their stories down.

I'm seeing this has become a lot about me, too. My stories. The way I look at the world and other people.

Working retail for so long jaded me a bit. I would tune people out, put my head down and stock shelves, do paperwork, let the other associates deal with questions and concerns.

I became even less of a people person.

If I'm really thinking about it, I needed to write this book.

Or maybe I'm fooling myself. Who can say?

Not sure if it's the rain or the heat making my head spin today and have these deep, heavy thoughts. Well, to me they're deep and heavy.

I have a couple of deadlines on some fiction stories, and might as well get my Dunkin visit in and, at the same time, get some work done.

Then I notice the guy in the corner is staring at me and he doesn't look too friendly.

Not that he's growling or shooting daggers with his eyes, he's just… really intense.

Intensely looking at me and seeing what I'm doing.

Two courses of action come to mind. I can put my head down and get back to work, creating brilliant stories that will someday change your life, or I can smile at the guy.

I'm not much of a smiler. In fact, if you see ninety-nine of a hundred pictures of me, there is no smile. Not something I do around anyone. I'm not sure why, either.

Before I realize what I'm doing, the sides of my mouth turn up and I hit this guy with a smile. Maybe a grin. Definitely not a sneer or a smirk.

A genuine friendly hello.

He looks confused and glances at his coffee, which he's still holding on the table with both hands like it's trying to escape.

I count silently to ten. He doesn't look at me again. I go back to working and listening to the rain on the window, the orders being run through the drive-thru and the employees working together. None of them are singing today.

I hear the Macarena and I feel like I've heard it in at least one other Dunkin Donuts this past week. Before this week, I can't remember the last time I'd heard the song. Honestly… not a fan, although I can say that for most music released after about 1990.

Speaking of Dunkin Radio: there are two DJ's, although that's not really the right word. Maybe on-air personalities? Anyway, the jump in after every few songs and either do a skit about what's new at Dunkin, or they toss out some trivia and facts about random stuff.

(add some of the trivia here, maybe look it up)

Back to the guy in the corner, who is now cleaning up and getting ready to leave. The garbage can is close to me, near the door. He hesitates as he approaches, as if I'm going to bite or talk to him.

I say hello because now it's really feeling awkward.

He nods, very non committal, but then his eyes lock on my bookmarks.

I always have a small stack of the bookmarks I made for the event, with the book cover, page address for the information and my email.

He points at the stack. No words. Just the finger-point.

"I'm writing a book about people I meet in Dunkin Donuts," I tell him.

"Why?"

I shrug my shoulders and smile. "Why not? People are interesting to talk to."

He really seems to be pondering this, eyes locked on the bookmarks.

I move my hand slowly so I don't frighten him, pick up a bookmark and offer it to him.

He doesn't take it. Now he's looking at me.

I wonder how many more of these awkward encounters I'll be having this month.

"Like… a real book?" Now he's looking at me.

I nod and smile. "Yes, sir."

"How much?"

"How much what?"

He frowns and I think I'm going to lose him. "How much will the book cost? Sometimes books are a lot of money. People price them too high, thinking they're worth more than they're really worth."

I'm not sure where he's going with this. "I'm not sure how much it will be priced yet. It depends on the word count, the page count, and what a distributor will want so they can sell it and make a profit."

"All about the profit," he mumbles but it isn't sarcastic or nasty. It's just a fact he's reciting. "Good luck with your book. I'll buy a copy when it comes out."

I'm still holding the bookmark in my hand.

He doesn't give me or the bookmark another look and is out the door, into the driving rain.

I stay longer than normal because I'm hoping the rain will slow down enough I can get to my car without getting soaked, and the roads are treacherous with all the rain.

Thirty minutes later and it's still coming down like cats and dogs, which is such an odd saying.

I see no cats and no dogs and I'm fine with it.

After finishing a chapter on one of my books, I decide to pack it in and run to my car.

I get soaked. Water running down my back. Shirt sticking to me. My goatee heavy with water.

As I pull out of the parking lot the rain stops suddenly and the sun shines as if it never rained.

If I'd waited another minute…

Wednesday October 9th

3430 University Boulevard South, Jacksonville FL at 11am

Large cold brew coffee with mocha

A stand-alone location I don't think I've ever been inside. I'm almost positive I've gone through the drive-thru. When I started looking at the Dunkin locations in the Jacksonville area, I was amazed at how many I'd visited since moving to town a few years ago.

How many I've passed a bunch of times and never stopped for whatever reason, too.

Today I've set up another interview with someone I know.

Tyler is a fellow baseball fan and we met at a Jacksonville Jumbo Shrimp game.

He's a talented guy who does custom baseball cards and pictures in his spare time, and I used to see them on my Instagram and decided to reach out and see what his deal was. Did he do it for profit? Was he one of the people I saw at every baseball game lugging around backpacks filled with sports cards, trying to get signatures from the players to later resell on eBay, or to collect for themselves?

It turns out I had already seen Tyler at a few games in that crowd, standing as close to the dugout as they could get, with card and pen in hand for the players.

I asked him how he started getting into not only the autograph stuff but customizing his own cards and photos.

"It started out in two parts. I was finding out some of the players, especially those who hadn't been in the game long and/or weren't prospects, didn't have a card or they might have one or two. Or a guy was a high-prized prospect with multiple cards that were all very expensive and it didn't make financial sense for me to buy them. A player that everyone was interested in might have cards starting at a dollar and up per card, and some of the time they might be over ten dollars for a single card. Even at a dollar a card, if you want to get the signatures of ten or fifteen guys, that's ten or fifteen dollars. I never sell my cards. I do it for myself. I like the story of it all, meeting the player and getting the keepsake for my private collection."

And that's when the idea of making your own cards came in?

"Yes. Not only would I save a ton of money, but I'd have something unique and very personal in my collection. I'm not selling them. It's a fun hobby to me."

What about the players who see the card? Do they ask where you got it?

"About half of the players will ask about it. Most of them want a card or two but they won't ask for it. If I can tell they're excited about the card, I'll take the initiative and ask them if they want a few. A lot of times my cards are the first time they've seen themselves on a card, or they like my design better than what's commercially out there. I'll bring a few to the next game I'm at and give them to the player. I used to assume they were all going to be interested, and I'd immediately try to give them a few, but a lot of guys weren't interested for whatever reason. Now I try to read the player's reaction to see first."

I find that not all players care about being on a baseball card, which blew my mind. From the players that I've grown to know over the last few years being in the stands, having players live with us and being the Booster Club president this past year, they usually get fifty of their cards from the companies to hand out, keep or do whatever they want with them. I've had players hand me ten cards because they don't want them, or players who will sign one for me but are excited to have so many to give out to friends and family. It just depends on the player.

How did Tyler get involved with customizing cards to begin with?

"On Facebook there are various groups I'm in and follow, and I'd see guys posting custom cards for everyone to see. I thought they looked great and I wished I could also do it. So I started to research it and I got Photoshop. I watched a lot of YouTube videos to see the different techniques and get ideas about how to make my own. It just took a lot of time and practice to start getting comfortable making them well enough to show them to anyone. I'd see some great ones on Instagram and want to figure out how they did certain things. It's really fun to do and it's such a unique story for me and the player. I'm hoping they see it and I get a great reaction from them. It's the main reason I collect. Some players are great to talk to and it's the perfect icebreaker to have a lasting conversation, or future conversations with them. You never know until you try."

Honestly... when I first saw Tyler's work I thought it was really good, but in the last two years or so I'm seeing new techniques and better cards and photos. It's cool to see him progressing with them. He's given us a few over the last couple of seasons, and we always ask for two of each. That way we can keep one for ourselves, usually after the player signs it for us, and give the player the other copy. Every player that's lived with us has received a unique photo thanks to Tyler. They're always very excited about it, and when I explain who did it, they usually know who Tyler is. Most of the time they'll already have had interaction with Tyler because he's already done a card for them.

Tyler doesn't just go to Jacksonville Jumbo Shrimp games to do cards and photos, either.

"Yeah. Baseball is my number one but I also do college football. Growing up a Florida State fan and going to Florida State for school, it was natural for me to start doing cards and photos for those players, too. It goes back to being a fan and collecting something unique. I've also done it for the Jacksonville Jaguars. Me and my dad had season tickets. I even met my wife at a game. My son is getting into hockey so we go to the Jacksonville IceMen games. The goal is to get some cool personal stories out of each interaction with the players."

When did he become a baseball fan?

"It was 1989. We were at a Captain D's, a seafood restaurant chain. They gave out a baseball card set. I remember having no clue what the cards were. My dad did. He followed baseball and started to explain who the players were and the teams they were on. I went home and started watching games with my dad. Whatever game was on. I'd watch WGN and the Cubs and rooted for them because they were on TV. I started to collect cards and my dad would give me the newspaper every morning so I could see the scores and stats. From there I started to really get into baseball, and when my dad told me the story of the Atlanta Braves going from last to first in the 1991 season, and I could watch them on TBS, I was hooked. I became a Braves fan and started following them. In 1991 I couldn't stay awake and fell asleep but my mom woke me to tell me they won. The following year, in '92, my parents took me to a spring training game. I saw other kids getting autographs but I didn't have cards or anything on me, so I took some sticky pad sheets we had in the car and got them signed. I still have them."

I'm looking forward to seeing Tyler around the Baseball Grounds in 2020 and what new tricks he can come up with for cards and photos. He's even made me a couple of my own baseball cards I proudly display in my office.

Thursday October 10th

2123 West Evans Street, Florence SC at 6:30 pm

Large hot Signature Latte caramel craze

medium iced coffee with French vanilla (my wife)

We're on the road and have made some good time today, heading to Haverhill in Massachusetts for a book signing on Saturday. It's an eighteen to twenty hour drive, so we're leaving a couple of days early and taking our time. The goal today is getting about half of the drive done and the other half tomorrow so we're nice and refreshed Saturday morning when I (hopefully) sell a hundred books.

Instead of stopping at a Dunkin on the way out of town, I opt to make a giant cup of Dunkin at home and start with that.

I'm obsessed with coffee. In case you hadn't guessed that yet. At one point I had a coffee maker on the counter next to a Keurig. In the morning I'd make a pot of coffee so I could drink and write all day, and then in the evening I'd pull out a K-cup and have a last cup of coffee.

While we were on one of our many trips this year, my wife spied one of the greatest inventions of all-time: a coffee maker on the left with a K-cup machine on the right.

Genius.

Now I can flip back and forth with ease, it takes up a lot less counter space, and if I'm in a rush to go somewhere I don't need to waste time making half a pot of coffee and wasting it.

My wife is not a coffee drinker.

In a show of solidarity or just because she knows we'll need to stop at many Dunkin stores on this and future trips this month, she decides to get an iced coffee but with French vanilla in it, as much as humanly possible. She wants to kill the coffee taste.

She's happy as she sips it. If she orders a non-coffee drink sometimes she'll swear she can taste coffee, but when I taste it I don't. Not sure if it's in her head, if my tastebuds are different, or if she's messing with me to get a reaction.

"How's this work?" She's sitting with me in comfy chairs near the window and there aren't a lot of people inside right now. At one of the bigger tables, a woman is tutoring a group of four children in what sounds like math. I try to tune it out because, you know… math.

"I make eye contact with people and if they seem interested I talk to them. Try to get their story. Ask them what they do… not what they do for a living. You see the difference?"

She doesn't seem convinced. She starts looking at her phone.

A teenager, not part of the study group, sneezes behind me. I bless him, the proper thing to do. He thanks me. Maybe it gives me a weak opening to talk to him… nope, he's got his backpack on his shoulder and slips out the side door.

"Talk to the lady at the counter," my wife says, not looking up from her phone. "She seemed really nice."

She was very nice, but she was also busy doing other things now. These employees are always keeping busy. Ideally, one of them would come out from behind the counter or the kitchen area to wipe down some tables or sweep the floor or maybe just be on break, and I could bother them for a couple of minutes. I don't want to get anyone in trouble.

I've been to this location before. Back in July, while driving to Rhode Island for a writer's meetup. I picked up fellow author Jay Wilburn as I headed north and I know I stopped here. I used the drive-thru that time. I usually always use the drive-thru.

Inside is nice and clean. Cheery with some Halloween decorations and nice and bright.

My wife is enjoying just sitting and playing on her phone, but I'm getting antsy.

Usually, I'll start writing. I have the tablet out and ready to go, but it feels weird with her next to me.

I'm feeling the pressure to either start writing or pack it up and head out the door.

"Whenever you're ready," I mumble.

"I'm fine." I believe she's either looking at strange videos people are posting or strange memes people are posting.

I watch the study group as a mom comes in to pick up her son. Maybe I can make eye contact with the smiling woman in yoga pants, but then I think it would be creepy with my wife next to me. I don't want to be *that* guy.

Suddenly I can't concentrate on writing. I don't even remember what I'm working on, even though the tablet is open to a story and all I need to do is read it.

I forget how to read.

My wife glances at me before her eyes go back to her phone.

"I'm ready to go," I say.

"Whenever you want." Her fingers are flying on her phone. Maybe she's texting her best friend to tell her how lame I am, staring into space and not really working.

Does she think this is what I really do? I sit in a Dunkin every day and stare at people like I'm nuts?

Wait… is it actually what I've been doing?

This is all so confusing. I imagine I'm starting to sweat, although there is no proof of it… like sweat on me anywhere.

I smile at the woman behind the counter, but she's working and doesn't notice me.

One of the kids is looking at me instead of doing his math work, and I can't blame him. Even staring at a guy who thinks he's sweating but isn't really sweating has to be more fun than math.

I look at my tablet screen again and sigh. I try to sigh dramatically but it isn't enough to get my wife's attention. Maybe she'll distract me. We can have a conversation.

She's smiling at something on her phone. I hope it isn't a cat meme. I can't even say why I'd disapprove.

Finally, I can't take it anymore. I've only taken a few sips of my latte but I'm ready to go. I close up the tablet, make sure to leave two of the bookmarks on the table, and clear my throat.

My wife is staring at me now, cat memes abandoned.

"You ready?" I ask.

"Whenever you're ready," she says. "Don't you have to talk to someone?"

"Not always," I say.

She gives me a look that lets me know she's either confused, she knows I'm lying, or both.

We leave and I nearly collide with the mom in her yoga pants in my race to the car.

Friday October 11th

14200 Smoketown Road, Woodbridge, VA at 9am

Small hot coffee, Britney Spears
Bacon, egg and cheese on cinnamon raisin bagel

large iced coffee with french vanilla (wife)
sausage, egg and cheese on a croissant (wife)

No drive-thru, busy but moving, a mix of people late for work and moms with kids late for school. My wife is asking me about Christmas presents, which means she knows what she wants and will try to slip it into conversation in the coming days. I need to be listening or else I'll end up buying her dish towels.

Wait. I think she wants dish towels. Married life is so hard sometimes.

I tell her about my dream, where we were at a school function and had to take our socks and shoes off, and then walked out into the parking lot without them. When we realize we're barefoot, and the ground is uneven and filled with small pebbles and maybe glass shards, she decides to go back inside for our shoes.

I decide to walk across the parking lot, barefoot, because… I have no idea. It's a dream.

The walk feels like it takes forever and I stumble a few times, hurting my feet as I try to walk. Cars navigate around me. My car keeps getting further and further away. The school parking lot is now the size of a parking lot for a baseball game, and we've parked in the last spot away from the stadium.

I get in the car and start it and drive back to the entrance and park the car.

And then I wait.

And wait.

Wait some more.

I'm even impatient in my dreams. It feels like forever and I keep seeing people leaving the building, all wearing shoes.

A police officer pulls up nearby and he gets out of his vehicle and nods at me.

Now I'm in panic mode in my dream. Not because I've done anything wrong, but because I am operating a motorized vehicle without shoes on. I know I'm going to get arrested.

As always happens, I wake up and when I get back to sleep the dream changes to something completely different. I'll never know if my wife ran off with my shoes.

I tell her I don't want anything for Christmas. Just being with her is a present enough. I mean it, too, whether she believes me or not.

She smiles and then tells me a couple of things she's been looking at.

We're still on the road and heading north toward Haverhill.

This will be our big stop for the day until dinner, wherever that ends up being.

No rush. No definite number of miles to put under our belts before we get there, although we should be in New England and the relative area we need to be in before nightfall if all goes as planned.

Even without the pressure of my wife being with me, I know there will be no interviews today. I've caught everyone in a rush like I said before. No one is mean, but they're not going to stop and chat. Usually I might get lucky with someone retired, or someone with a rare Friday off, but not today.

I give it a shot anyway, while my wife is taking care of work emails on her phone.

I smile as people come in and know my smile might be creepy. I hardly ever smile, and it isn't because I'm not happy. It's because I've never really smiled in pictures or in life. It's a weird habit (I call it a habit, others might call it lunacy) I've had forever, even as a kid. Of course I laugh a lot. I do smile occasionally when I'm not thinking about it or think there isn't a camera pointing at me.

Some people return my smile but most are too busy to notice the weird dude with the weird smile. Maybe they've all been taught from a young age not to engage with weird people.

I get a couple of nods from working men and I feel good about it, even though I wouldn't last a day doing whatever it is they do: construction. Landscaping. Bullfighting. Whatever manly thing they're going to do today after the coffee has kicked in.

I wonder how in shape I'd be if I had gotten into manual labor instead of retail. I imagine I'd be much lighter and muscular. Maybe I wouldn't have lost my hair. Maybe I'd have my own construction show on TV right now.

As I smile at a woman leaving with her two kids a funny thing happens: she stops like she either knows me or wants to know me. A stutter-step before she suddenly needs to talk to her daughters and race out the door.

Did she think I was checking her out? Did I make her day because maybe she thought I was checking her out? Is my wife going to kill me for smiling at another woman? She was pretty but I wasn't flirting. I was trying to get her attention and see if she wanted to chat.

About what? A date? With her kids? This is all too much for me to handle. I'm a wreck inside, over-thinking everything as usual.

I thought having my wife with me would make it easier. I'd be forced into talking with someone. She'd give me the push to start a conversation, something I'm horrible at.

Instead, I feel like every time I look at another woman she'd judging me, which makes no sense. I'm not flirting and I'm not checking anyone out. I'm happily married and love my life.

The problem? I need to stop trying to be smiley to everyone. It's unnatural. I'm not the smiling kinda guy. I'm learning this and so much more about me.

Like how self-conscious I am staring at people with my wife at the table, likely wondering what I'm doing.

"Are you going to talk to someone?" She asks nicely, not condescending, not threatening, no sense of rush to either talk to someone or get her out of there. She seems to be enjoying the cat memes and videos of people falling, and is relaxed.

"I'm going to… if someone wants to." I say it as if I've put it out into the ether, and someone will magically pick up on my words and want to suddenly talk to the guy in the corner who is either smiling like a creep or not frowning like someone who's mad.

I spent what feels like the next five hours, but is probably only five minutes, watching the crowd. Getting the vibe. Realizing no one is interested in chatting with me, and I'm too chicken to approach someone in a rush to get their coffee and bagel and hit the road.

"I'm ready when you are," I say, and get up. This is harder than it looks.

"You sure?" Now I think she's feeling pity for me. Like I'm a failure at this. Maybe she thinks this book will be awful, full of blank pages or lame observations about people I never actually talked to.

Now I'm wondering if this is exactly what this book is going to end up.

I also wish I'd ordered a bigger coffee, because a small isn't going to last too much longer, especially riding in the car.

I've learned how neurotic I am when it comes to me being outside my house.

My wife must really love me, or she's insane to be with someone like me.

I make a mental note to show her tomorrow I can be a normal human being and have a normal conversation with someone other than her.

Fingers crossed.

Saturday October 12th

8 Stiles Road, Salem, NH at 8:30am

Small hot coffee, cream and sugar
Plain bagel with cream cheese

Large iced coffee with mocha (for my wife)
Plain bagel with strawberry cream cheese (my wife again)

We spent the night in Salem but in New Hampshire. Not Massachusetts, where the witches were burned. OK, I think only a couple were actually killed that way. I'm going to be honest: I didn't even know there was a Salem in NH, so I think the old adage 'all publicity is good publicity' worked out well for the MA version. I know, as a kid, we got to visit Salem to see where the witch trials were and all the touristy things associated with it.

There is a Dunkin Donuts on this side of the border, but let's be honest... Dunkin rules in New England. You can't go too far without seeing the familiar color scheme.

We have several choices for locations but choose this one, which is about a mile from the hotel.

This is one of the things I miss about living in the north. Besides having an actual change of seasons, it's a beautiful fifty degrees and it makes me want a hot coffee and a bagel while I watch the leaves change.

The staff here is so fast I feel like I'm not even done ordering and I already have my order in hand. They are that quick. We sit inside and there's no time to talk with anyone coming in and out because orders are being placed and filled so rapidly I wonder if the woman making the coffees already knows who's coming in and what they will order.

Perhaps she's psychic or has superhuman powers. Maybe she's been birthed in a secret Dunkin lab where they make super-employees who can pour fifty-seven large coffees at once.

Maybe she just loves her job and wants to keep the train rolling nice and fast.

I want to talk with her but, despite her smile, she is on fire. In the zone. She has one eye on her pour and the other on the orders, listening in as they're being placed.

If I didn't have a book signing to go to I'd sit and watch her for hours, waiting for the big rushes were it's more than just a steady stream of customers and a raging river of them.

When I leave I want to kick myself for not at least getting her name.

That's been the conundrum for me, too: not wanting to bother an employee while they're working. I'm sure during off hours, when the rush isn't as intense as this, I could pull someone aside and try not to make an idiot of myself explaining what I'm doing and why.

Maybe before the month is out? Probably not.

My wife seems to be getting into this more, pointing out which employees are flying behind the counter and how quickly orders are being placed, no matter what customers want.

I know I couldn't do it. Not with so many different food items to be put together. Add in drinks, both hot and cold, and everything else. Enough to make my head spin.

I wonder if, in the beginning, it was just a couple of easy choices: hot coffee and a few different donuts to choose from.

I wonder if I could've even handled that.

My wife points out a few locals coming and going, and we make up stories about them to pass the time while we eat our bagels and drink our coffees.

We leave only because I have a book signing to go to at the Haverhill Public Library, along with dozens of other authors.

It turns out to be a great afternoon, I sell a few books, meet a few new readers, and one of the highlights is not only when the woman running the event asks if we'd like coffee, but says she's heading to Dunks.

Not Dunkin Donuts. Not Dunkin.

Dunks, which strikes my wife as funny.

The woman says Dunks several times before she disappears to get said Dunks.

I continue to sell books and talk with some authors from the New England area I never get to see in person.

Then suddenly there is hot coffee for everyone to enjoy.

Sorry… I mean Dunks.

Afterward, we head to a local restaurant, where a lot of the authors take over the upper floor and have a big meal before heading off to our own areas of the country.

It was a blast and I hope to be invited back next year.

179 Littleton Road, Westford, MA at 7:30pm

Large frozen coffee (with whipped cream)
2 glazed donuts

Large iced coffee with caramel swirl (wife)

On our way south from a very successful book signing in Haverhill, we had to stop at a Dunkin in Massachusetts. Felt like the right thing to do, and I needed a nice kick for the five hour drive to New Jersey for the next book signing.

This stop was at a gas station, although it isn't like the ones we see in Florida or the south, where it's just a few trays of donuts and you can make your own coffee.

An actual setup of a Dunkin, with full menu and everything that goes with it, greets us, along with a smiling young woman who keeps her calm even when I start in on the bad dad jokes and try to be funny.

I won't repeat them. You've likely heard all of them from your dad, anyway.

The fact I order and devour two donuts while my wife says she only wants a drink doesn't faze me at all. I'm fat. Plump. A big guy who enjoys the finer things in life, like glazed donuts. They are like little clouds of love, and I want them all in my large belly.

I'm enjoying the trip and seeing new places and new Dunkin locations. As I wait for my order, a group of local kids wanders in and starts ordering a crazy amount of coffee and donuts. There are seven teenagers but they order four dozen donuts and an iced drink each. Then they add in some bagels with cream cheese, a couple of apple fritters and some other stuff. I was trying to be nosy but my wife grabbed our drinks and led me outside like I was a little kid, trying to see what the adults were doing.

Usually she's all for people-watching, but it was going to be a long drive south to New Jersey tonight, where we still had to find a hotel, too.

And since I hardly ever drove, preferring to ride shotgun and periodically fall asleep so she could listen to country music while I snored… she was the driver and she owned the road.

So far, nearly two weeks into this grand odyssey, I'm having a blast. Even though I'm not chatting with a lot of people, I'm able to enjoy myself. Just being out of the house is a nice twist for me. Observing others as they go about their day, getting the small ten-minute snapshot, is fun.

I imagine a few of these people will end up in a future story I'll write, too. There's nothing better for fiction than meeting real people and using their nonfiction for a story. If that makes any sense.

It does to me, and that's what is on my mind a few miles down the road, as I begin to fade out.

My wife shakes her head, switches to country music, and I am fast asleep, dreams of selling books and drinking Dunkin coffee swirling in my dreams.

Sunday October 13th

216 Route 35, Point Pleasant, NJ at 10am

large dark roast iced coffee with cream and sugar
apple fritter
sesame bagel with cream cheese

large hot coffee with French Vanilla (wife)
apple fritter (wife)
warm bagel twist (wife)

We decided more was better and kept one-upping each other on added items. Or we used it as an excuse to each get a second edible item to eat.

I'd never had an apple fritter from Dunkin, but now I know what the most important thing I've learned writing this book is: I need to eat more of their apple fritters.

I've been to this location numerous times in the last five years. Every trip back to New Jersey during a book signing tour usually gets me into this area because of my good friend, George.

I've known him since third grade, which (if you're doing the math) was about a hundred and twenty-two years ago. Maybe less.

The location doubles as a Baskin Robbins as well. It's big and spacious with quite a few tables for customers, and this morning they had a steady stream of them, mostly there to get a coffee on their way to doing something fun with the family on a Sunday morning.

My wife and I acted like they didn't offer delicious ice cream a few feet away from where we ordered our drinks and food, because we had already ordered more than enough and we had a long day ahead of us. Book signing in nearby Eatontown. Lunch with the other authors and friends. Then the long drive south toward home.

Jorge was mopping at this location. I don't know the young man. I never talked to him. Barely made eye contact, as he was into his work. Again, it's a big location. Lots of floor space. Lots of mopping to be done. If it wasn't for his focus on getting the floor cleaned I would've bothered him for a quick interview, but then I'd feel guilty if he got behind.

I'm noticing something about Dunkin: either their managers are hiding in the back room or they're also on the floor working with the staff. I feel like it's usually been the latter, because there's always someone who's keeping everything flowing. As I watch each location, I know the managers are out there taking and creating orders for customers. It's a fast-paced business, and if it gets behind you'll have a lot of irate people who just want a quick cup of coffee.

In my experience in retail, that isn't always the manager, either. A lot of times the workers will step up and keep it going for a few reasons: pride in their work, just being happy to accomplish something today, or ownership.

When I say ownership it comes from experience. Every place I've ever worked at that I feel ownership is special. It means I'm not the owner but I'm treating it like I am. It goes beyond pride. When you feel ownership in where you work, you have the sense that every penny saved, every dollar earned, is on you… but in a good way. You're not getting to work and stressing about these things or leaving after your shift and worrying. It just means that while you're in the building every customer is treated as special, every system in place is followed and taught to the new employees by example, and you share a genuine smile.

So far, in my travels, I can honestly say I haven't heard a negative word or seen a grumpy employee. I imagine, if I wasn't already on my career path, I might be tempted to work at a place like this… but not this location, about a thousand miles from my home in Florida. The commute would be awful.

I make sure to give Jorge a nod as we leave, and leave him to his work.

I'm tired after the drive last night and having to find a motel to stay in last night, and I know my wife is exhausted from being up until we got the room. Now we'll go to a bookstore and try to sell some books, while also getting to see some of my author buddies again.

It is a beautiful day out. Warm and sunny.

Not a great day to sell books.

It doesn't matter, though. I am back in New Jersey, even if only for a few hours. Back where I was born and raised.

Today we sell books and then we hit the road south.

Fingers crossed I sell a few books.

Monday October 14th

908 Market Street, Emporia, VA at 9am

Large iced Signature Latte with cocoa mocha chocolate chip muffin

Large iced latte with French vanilla (wife) chocolate chip muffin (wife)

Another location inside a gas station, it had a few tables and a counter near the window where we sat. The family in front of us ordered half a dozen drinks and a dozen donuts, although they each placed an order for two donuts. My wife commented they should've ordered a dozen and filled the box, but she only said it to me.

I wonder how many customers do this: instead of going in order of who knows what they want and the fact they'll all be ordering donuts and should buy them by the dozen instead of two at a time and a drink... sorry. Long day of driving. I just want to order.

The employee is smiling and chatting while keeping the line moving quickly, and despite the children ordering intricate drinks and changing the order a couple of times each, they cranked out the orders and I was ready to order myself.

That's when the panic set in.

Not only was the entire menu in a strange language I couldn't read, but I had no idea what coffee was. What anything was.

Okay, maybe it wasn't that bad. I tend to exaggerate. I did really panic, though, because I couldn't remember what drinks I had ordered so far this month. What combinations had been tossed into a cup and consumed by yours truly.

I ordered and as soon as I got my drink I had to scroll through the chapters to see if I screwed up. I wondered what I'd do if I had ordered an item again. Would the month be over? Would I have lost? Lost what? Why was I over-thinking this?

The chocolate chip muffin was delicious. Not dry like some muffins can be. There is nothing worse than a dried-out muffin, a husk of parchment-like innards. It was delicious and woke me up, settled me down after the family ordering and ordering like they'd never been inside a Dunkin or any public building that sold items.

I watched people coming and going, pumping their gas. Sipped on my latte.

Here's a funny thing about me: before this exciting monthly journey, I rarely had anything except hot coffee. I am not a huge fan of ordering a flavor or anything fancy when I'm out. I prefer a typical large hot coffee, Britney Spears. On occasion I'll have an iced coffee, Britney Spears.

Now I'm trying latte, macchiato, cold brew and different flavors in my drink.

I am truly a wild man.

As a full-time writer, I take for granted everyone else having something to do like leave the house and go to work. Having an actual job that hands you a paycheck at the end of the week, or twice monthly. An agreed-upon amount per hour.

Writing means going for days, weeks or sometimes months without a steady stream of cash coming in. Unfortunately, we're not all making King, Patterson and Koontz money.

I wouldn't give it up for my life, though. Being able to do something I've wanted to do since I was twelve, and make a living at it? Priceless.

Of course, a big payday once in awhile would help offset all the money I spend on my career, too. I know it's tough on my wife as the main breadwinner. She is responsible for the mortgage, the phone bill, the electric and the food and gas. I'm tossing my few dollars into the pile every month (when it comes in) and trying to sneak away before she figures out what a money-suck being married to me is.

Except... she loves me. She supports me. It isn't about the money, although I'd love to make a lot of it. This is all about being happy, living the best life we can, and being happy being together on unique trips like this.

It's also about the latte and muffins today, too.

1457 Bells Highway, Walterboro, SC at 3pm

Large vanilla chai coolatta with whipped cream

My wife didn't order anything. I'm not sure if she's all French vanilla'd out or she just can't hang with me at Dunkin each day. Who can say?

The employee taking my order has on orange eyeshadow to go with the Dunkin motif and the

Halloween decor. Or maybe she wears it all year long. She might be a big fan of orange.

She's pleasant and smiles a lot. I don't smile nearly enough, even though I'm a relatively happy guy. Once we sit down and I start writing and my wife starts answering emails on her phone, Orange Eye Shadow starts telling one of the other employees about her weekend and how burnt she got at the beach.

I don't miss retail but I do miss interacting with fellow employees. Hearing about their families and their drama. The good and the bad. It helped to pass hours each day waiting for another story. Even when I was a full-time retail manager working six days and over seventy hours a week, I still wrote stories whenever I had a free moment. These daily conversations seeped into a lot of my fiction.

Sometimes I get so into writing at home I forget I need to be around actual people. If my wife is working late a few nights in a row, I tend to never stop working until she comes home. It means long hours, maybe as many as when I worked retail.

Except I love every minute of this. Writing, publishing and promoting twelve to fifteen hours a day seven days a week is awesome.

Maybe not for my wife, though. It takes a special kind of person to get up every morning and have to get dressed and go out into the real world and interact with people you might not want to interact with. And you do it while your partner (in this case, me) gets to sit around in his pajamas and drink coffee and ignore the world while he makes up things for a living.

Not everyone is creative or can create fiction, music, or whatever is in their heads and needs to come out. My wife is a number person. Give her a spreadsheet and a math problem and she will dive into it with as much glee as I have when writing a scene in a book.

A large group of kids comes in and I'm an old man so I expect trouble. They're loud and laughing and… just having fun. They're being goofy, maybe freshmen in high school, if I can still judge that. They seem to have no cares in the world. It's a Monday afternoon. School has probably just let out. They're making the trek over to a Dunkin to share a dozen donuts and talk about the bright future ahead of them.

This is the stuff I miss by sitting home by myself in my pajamas. Real people doing real things. A part of me thinks I should go and introduce myself, see if they want to be interviewed for the book. See if I can get some insight into how the young kids do things these days. Be a hip dude with some funky moves… I imagine the kids don't talk like that today. Heck, when I was their age we didn't talk like that.

Of course, there's no way I'm getting up and going over in front of my wife. She'll think I'm crazy. Yeah, that's the excuse I came up with. In reality, when she reads this she'll ask me why I didn't go over and strike up a conversation. To her it seems like a simple thing to do. For me… not so much.

The kids are harmless and enjoying the freedom of getting out of school and having their lives ahead of them. I envy their naivety and energy. Was I like that at their age? Probably not. I was always fretting and worrying about the little things. The small stuff I couldn't even remember now. Probably couldn't remember a week or so after it was a thought in my teenage head.

Orange Eye Shadow is going on about her weekend to the other girl working, and they're comparing notes as to where the best places to get a suntan are, which place has the best pizza and a hundred other random thoughts to pass the time working.

After writing for a bit and knowing I'm never going to talk to anyone, I start to pack it all up.

My wife glances at me, as if to say *another Dunkin you're not going to talk to anyone in,* or maybe she's just ready to hit the road, too.

I make a promise I know I can't keep to start interacting more with people as soon as we get home, and my wife isn't with me. It's easy to blame her for my insecurities and the reason I'm not chatting amiably with anyone.

As if that was the reason. As if she isn't going to likely frown when she reads this.

We get back on the road and another few hours of driving south to Florida.

Tuesday October 15th

11657 Beach Boulevard, Jacksonville FL at 3pm

Large sweet tea with lemon wedges

Another location I've been to dozens of times but never gone inside. It's later in the afternoon, after the lunch rush but before everyone is leaving work to get home.

It's also good to be home from my trip. Back home for a few days until the next book signing event.

Once I caught up on flagged emails and the things I put off to the side before we left, I hit the road. It was much easier going twenty minutes away, rather than twenty hours.

I'm not the only customer in the building. There's a guy who's interviewing a younger guy for a possible job. I'm trying to be casual and listen in because I'm nosy. I think the company is driving trucks or delivery items in town. Maybe waste removal? I wonder how awkward it would be to interrupt them.

They are interrupted because the interviewer knocks his large coffee off the table and it goes everywhere. He's apologetic to the guy who works here and has to mop it up.

Once they get back to the interview I can tell he's at first flustered, trying to figure out which questions he's already asked or what answers he's received.

I enjoyed interviewing people for work. There's an art to asking questions and getting body language and direct eye contact from potential employees and figuring out what their real answer is. It always amazed me when someone coming into an interview would tell you all the bad things they'd done in the past, or act like they didn't even want the job.

You feel sorry for the interviewees who you're not going to hire or the ones who can't pass a background check or whatever simple computer test they need to take to get the job.

I've had some really great interviews with people putting their best foot forward, but as soon as they start working the drama kicks in. Suddenly they can't work any shift, even though in the interview and in their paperwork they said they could. The reliable transportation they promised to have? Yeah, that was only to get to the interview. They live twenty miles away and there isn't a bus that they can ride to work. They also forgot to tell me they start classes in two weeks or the big family reunion in Wenona is the first weekend I have them on the schedule.

I miss the interview process. Maybe not when they start working.

The guy being interviewed leaves and another guy, who's been sitting in the far corner paying attention, stands and goes to the table. Back to back interviews at the same spot and they're overlapping. Maybe the coffee spill really threw the interviewer off his game.

He goes through the questions in his head in the same basic order and this guy being interviewed isn't smiling as much as the last guy. His body language is slightly off. He's nervous but there's more. Maybe he's hiding something.

And then my mind wanders and I start to dream up scenarios for a book I had no idea I needed to write until this moment. It's the curse of being creative and unable to stop it when the brain kicks in and ideas won't leave you alone.

When I was a younger writer I used to write down every little idea that came into my head. I carried a small notebook in my back pocket, and wrote on napkins and sticky notes and anything else I could write on. I had piles of these ideas all over my bedroom. My goal was to somehow organize them. It would magically form the basis of the next thirty *New York Times* best sellers.

Days, weeks and months later I would pick up a random note, ready to begin on an epic novel excursion.

Man with hat in diner orders eggs.

Okay… maybe it meant something a few weeks ago, but now it means nothing. That isn't even a character in a story. That's someone you don't even mention. He's the out-of-focus background body in any TV show or movie.

Nowadays, I don't write any of it down. I keep it in my head and let it percolate. Simmer. Form into a fully-realized idea. Other ideas will graft to it if it's good enough. Other ideas in the future will be added to this kernel of a story, things that might not seem to go together.

Building blocks that form a real story. Readers and non-creative people think artists are always in search of ideas, as if they struggle to figure out what to work on next. In most cases (and especially with me) I have a million ideas swimming in my head. I need to find the time to write them all down. I will never run out of stories, even if I live to be two hundred.

What if I lived to be two hundred and had to write all these stories in order to stay alive? See. Story idea.

I feel sorry for the two employees working this afternoon, because one of them was manning the drive-thru and putting orders together while the other one had to mop the floor. There could be more people working here but I don't see them, unless they're in the kitchen. Maybe this is a change of shift time of day. Mopping up the floor takes a lot of time out of the one guy, although he's smiling as he works and waves off the guy who spilled the coffee who is embarrassed and wants to mop it himself.

I'm feeling so awkward watching I want to grab the mop and do it, but I know it's not gonna happen. It would make the guy who spilled the coffee feel worse, the guy working feel like I was telling him he isn't doing a good job, and then I'd have to actually exert myself and do something I don't like to do. No wins in any of this scenario.

I keep finding myself thinking about *what if's* instead of just doing and then talking about *what happened*. I'm seeing the pattern you've probably been seeing since the third or fourth day into this exercise. In a perfect world, by the end of this month, I'll have gotten the nerve to be a better person, someone who freely talks to others and shares ideas and a laugh, and faces and conquers my insecurities, fears and crippling antisocial behavior.

Spoiler alert: ain't gonna happen.

I'm saved by my phone ringing, and have a chat with Jim Cobb, who does the *Library At The End of The World* podcast. He's a prepper, survivalist and loves apocalyptic fiction. He's also very manly and outgoing.

I also love apocalyptic fiction and have a podcast. All other similarities are nonexistent.

By the time my phone call is done, the floor is mopped and pretty again, and the interviewer has left. I wonder which guy he ultimately hired, or if I missed a few interviews.

Such is life when you get a snapshot of what someone else is doing, and that tiny window into their day.

Wednesday October 16th

3031 Monument Road, Jacksonville FL at noon

Large hot green tea with sugar

I don't drink tea nearly enough, especially of the hot variety. Not sure why. I like it. Like coffee, when I was a kid it was an adult drink. Kids were supposed to drink tap water and the occasional soda when it was a special occasion. I think if I'd have started drinking tea in my late teens I would've been hooked instead of coffee? Nah. Probably not. I really, really like coffee. I can't get through a day without it, while I never remember to drink tea.

I've never been to this location. Didn't even know it existed. From the foot traffic I guess other people know it's here, because they're getting a steady stream of customers.

It's a decent size at the end of a strip mall, and the drive-thru is also steady. Plenty of seating and also window seating.

The normal amount of employees, and they're all busy as usual.

I'm beginning to feel, halfway through my journey, that I'll never get a proper interview with an employee. I'm fine with it. If I found one who wanted to sit and chat it would mean they probably weren't that great of a worker and part of the team.

Halfway through the month already. It's amazing to me how quickly this has been going. I thought it might drag having to leave the house each day and finding another location to drive to, order food and/or drink, and write and maybe talk to people.

I'm really enjoying this so far. I haven't had a day where I wanted to make up excuses not to put pants on and grab my car keys.

Local Jacksonville noir crime thriller author Michael Wiley wrote a book, *Monument Road*, and it is brilliant. Just a little plug for some good literature. As far as I can tell, this location has nothing to do with the story except being on the title road.

A young couple, half my age, gets their order and sits at the table right next to me despite there being a few empty spots. It's always odd to me when people in a place like this don't find the equidistant table away from everyone else. It's an unwritten rule that should be a law. X number of tables between you and whoever else is in the room.

Nope. They're right next to me. I have my head down writing and not making eye contact because I want to be left alone. So much for turning over a new leaf and engaging with others for the greater goal of this book.

Besides, I automatically assume I have nothing to talk to them about. They're young and won't get my references. I have children their age. They'll groan at my dad jokes and give me pitiful stares. They'll goof on me for days, a running joke shared between them.

I feel pathetic, over-thinking talking to another human being.

"You don't put ham on an English muffin," the woman said next to me, bringing me out of my self-defeating thoughts. "Sausage. Egg. Cheese. Only."

Her husband shook his head and smiled. "Ham. Nothing else. Egg and cheese goes on a croissant."

I'm not sure if he's arguing just to argue, if this is one of those in-jokes between them, a fun argument going back since the days they'd started dating, or if this was a new one. They were both wearing wedding rings and they had an ease I knew was the result of being married, and not two married people on a late lunch together. Maybe an early dinner? Nah. Only my parents and the few people older than me ate dinner this early. Some of them still called it supper, too.

She's waving her free hand dismissively and shaking her sandwich at him in a semi-threatening manner. "Ham on bread is so boring. At least put cheese on it."

He's shaking his head.

I put my hands back on the tablet keyboard but I can't concentrate. Their argument is in my head. I'm trying to decipher if this is them playing around or an actual argument. They're smiling but it feels like it's getting intense.

"What if you compromised and got ham, egg and cheese on a muffin?" She's no longer waving her food, having taken a large bite and putting it back down on her wrapper.

"Ham. Only." He's mimicking her, which will not award him any brownie points and likely a place on the couch tonight, alone and confused where he went wrong.

You went wrong by mimicking her, buddy.

I swear he looks like he's sweating now. "I love ham. Always have. I could eat ham on an English muffin. White bread. Wheat bread. In a pita." He names roughly seventy-five other food items to compliment his ham, most either weird, unknown or plain gross to me. This guy loves him some ham.

She's shaking her head as she takes another bite.

I realize too late I'm staring at her chewing.

As I try to turn away and go back to my writing, she catches my eye. I'm paralyzed. Is she going to yell at me now? I'm drinking tea. Surely I have nothing to add to this…

"You heard what we were saying," she says, but it isn't mad or annoyed. "Be honest… which one of us is wrong?"

I'm not sure there is a right and wrong and tell her so. She's not buying it.

"Me or him?"

"I prefer ham, egg and cheese on an English muffin," I say. Now I want to order food, too. Even though I've already had lunch today. As she smiles I put up a hand. "But, in all fairness, there's nothing wrong with just ham." I smile. "Unless it's Canadian ham."

The Canadian ham comment is a stupid joke, not really what I'm thinking. I have nothing against Canada or ham, or what they call Canadian ham. Don't they also call it Canadian bacon? It's all so confusing to me. Do they call our ham bacon and vice versa? Do all Canadians love Rush and Celine Dion? So many questions without answers.

"That isn't ham," she says, and now I think she's angry with me. "I'm talking about Keith only ordering ham no matter where we go."

Keith shrugs. "I like ham. Sue me."

"Do you order ham at fast food places?" I ask, knowing I need to mind my own business and turn away. I can't. I've been sucked into the debate.

Keith is nodding. "Whenever possible." He names three places off the top of his head that have ham in some form. He gets just ham as a pizza topping. He'll make a ham at home on the weekend and eat it for lunch and dinner over the next few days. Grilled ham on hamburger buns, although in fairness hamburger buns has ham in there, too.

"He never did this when we were dating," she says.

"Not true. I ate a lot of ham, but we were in college and it isn't like we lived together." He's looking at me now to plead his case. "My roommate's mom bought him cases of Ramen Noodle. My parents gave me cooked hams. Deli sliced ham. A loaf of bread. It's delicious. I'm not going to apologize for that. You get it, right?"

I can best be described as a deer in headlights as his wife turns her head to me, cocking it to the side. I've seen that same look from my wife.

My lips are sealed. No good can come from answering.

I wisely change the subject and tell them about my book, which they are both excited about.

"Are we going to be in the book?" She's smiling. "The crazy couple fighting about ham?"

"Yes," I say, hoping she doesn't tell me not to write about this.

"Cool," she says and I'm relieved. So is Keith.

"I never got your name," I say to her as they're getting up to leave. "For my book."

She is smiling but shaking her head. "I don't want anyone to know I'm with him. He's crazy. He puts ham on everything. I'm beginning to doubt this marriage."

Keith puts his arm around her. "It's built on ham and love."

"But not Canadian ham," I say as they leave.

I'm not sure what happened but I actually talked to someone, so it's a win for me.

Thursday October 17th

300 South Nova Road, Ormond Beach FL at noon

Chocolate creme filled donut
Strawberry frosted donut

This location is near my parents' house, and I used to come here all the time. But never inside. I realized again how much I relied on the drive-thru to get my daily fill of coffee and donuts.

I wonder, once the month is done, if I go back to my old ways and never go inside unless I need a dozen donuts.

This location's drive-thru is rocking with the lunch crowd. Inside there are only a few people, and most of them aren't staying long. Plus, with such a nice day outside, they're going to sit in the outside patio area to chat.

I'm inside at one of the handful of tables enjoying the air conditioning.

I would've been here a couple of hours sooner but I stopped off to see my parents. With so much travel lately, I haven't seen them in a few weeks and maybe talked to them twice or three times in the last month.

My wife calls me a mama's boy and I am. Proudly. There are times when I talk to her every day or at least every other day. I have to regale her with the trips we've taken or the books I'm selling. With my dad it's all about baseball and baseball cards.

Case in point: I have to show off the 1969 Topps Mickey Mantle card I recently bought at a card show, and what a great deal I got on the price. He studies the card and nods approvingly, but has to give his critique about it because he's my dad. Which is why I showed him the card to begin with.

We don't pull punches in my family. Tell it like it is. Jersey attitude.

I tell everyone I got my love of reading from my mother and the ability to make things up from my father. So far the combination has resulted in writing full-time and living my dream.

So, in case I haven't said it enough, mom and dad… Thank you.

I love the donuts and my worry when I started this was that I'd simply order two different donuts a day and be done with it. Even though I've mixed in a lot of sandwiches and bagels so far, my go-to will always be a donut.

This is actually a newer location in this area, as there was a Dunkin just up the road a block or two on a very busy intersection. I'd go there all the time when I first moved to Florida in 2001, but it was tough to get around and into the drive-thru lane without backing up traffic or having to be backed up.

The new location is much better for traffic and parking.

With each stop there are certain nuances I'm seeing. In this location most customers coming in are immediately leaving. Not many are sitting down to enjoy their purchases, at least today.

It's also a lot of single people. I mean, they might all be married, but single as far as there are only one of them. I guess people work for a living and are on lunch break right now? I have to stop and think about what day it is.

Thursday. You're welcome.

When I first get inside there's an older guy at the counter ordering. He has a Dunkin cup he wants filled with coffee and two donuts, which is what leads me to also order two donuts.

"Do you want both donuts in the same bag or keep them separate since they're both creme filled?"

He smiles at the question. "Put them in the same bag. I'm going to eat them in a second." The guy glances at me. "I've earned it."

I laugh. "I imagine you have."

He gets his coffee and donuts and takes a seat in a corner while I get my two donuts. I'm not asked if I want them in the same bag. I suppose I haven't earned it yet.

When I sit across from him I see he has a tablet out as well, furiously typing away on it. Much faster than I'll ever be able to type.

I am more a pecker than a typer.

Two fingered stabbing of the keyboard for me. If I could actually take the time to properly type I'd be dangerous. I took a typing class in high school but that was… well, a long, long time ago. If I'm working in a dark place, like a hotel room and my wife is sleeping so I don't want to turn on the light, I can put my hands in the proper position and actually type without having to stare at my hands.

But pecking with my two pointer fingers (that's what I call them) is comfortable for me.

The guy glances over at me, seeing me trying to type furiously and failing, and gives me a nod. I'm not sure if it's because I can't keep up with him or he has more experience in life and typing, or just because he's being friendly.

I have a tendency to overanalyze most situations. Like this one.

"You writing or searching?" the guy asks from across the room. He points at his tablet. "I'm searching."

"For what?" I ask, happy he engaged with me first so I don't have to build up to figuring an icebreaker to get him to open up.

"Vacation. Maybe a cruise. I'm not getting any younger," he says. "You ever been on a cruise?"

"I've been on a few. The last time was my honeymoon nearly five years ago. The next one will be an Alaskan cruise next year for our fifth anniversary," I tell him.

"I've never been, and my wife always wanted to go on one. I was always too busy with work and then with our kids." He suddenly looks sad. "She's gone and I swore I'd do a cruise." He grins and his face lights up. "I once told her to be careful what you wish for. If I had to do it on my own, some hottie half my age is going to scoop me up and take all my money."

"What did she say?"

He shrugged. "She told me, if I could find someone that young and stupid, to knock myself out. She already knows I'm stupid. Besides, the joke would be on my hottie because I'm barely getting by as it is." He held up three fingers. "Three years since she's been gone and I might have enough to book a cruise now. Three days to the Bahamas, maybe. I don't want to see the world. I've never even been to Canada. I like it here."

I've never been to Canada, either. We came close a couple of years ago, visiting Niagara Falls. It was breathtaking and I got really wet. I could see Canada on the other side, although it looked like a mirror image of the U.S. side to me.

He smiles as he types. "Booked." He blows out a breath, finishes his donut (I'd finished mine about eight seconds after I sat down) and closes his tablet. "Wish me luck."

"Getting your money stolen by a hottie?" I ask.

He shrugs and grins. "Yes."

I laugh. "Good luck."

250 South Atlantic Avenue, Ormond Beach FL

Large strawberry coolatta

I totally forgot it was Biketoberfest, and the street outside, which doubles for A1A, was busy with bikers. I used to live in the area. I already mentioned my parents still do. Even though I might look like a biker, I have no balance. Never been on a bike. They look really cool and I can imagine how cool my goatee flapping in the wind would look, but I'll stick to four wheels.

The run from up further north to Daytona Beach is always busy this time of year, and it's only Thursday. The weekend will be crazy packed.

I see one biker who isn't having fun, though. He's just been pulled over into the parking lot by a police officer on a motorcycle and is getting a ticket.

That will ruin a good bike event.

Getting pulled over on a bike looks awkward. Instead of sitting in your car while the officer goes back to his car to write you a ticket, you have to stand on the sidewalk and watch him, standing at the back of his bike, writing your ticket. In the Florida sun.

Being in your leather and gear in the heat might be worse than the ticket. The guy looks annoyed but he's got his back to the police officer and is watching the other bikers ride by, not getting a ticket. There is more than one nod from a sympathetic biker, too. It's a brotherhood I will never be able to join unless I can suddenly figure out the magic of being balanced.

It reminds me of a previous Biketoberfest, when my kids were little. I'd taken the family to a restaurant near the Daytona Speedway. The place was packed with bikers. I was wearing a black t-shirt and a red bandana on my head, which I used to do all the time. I thought I looked good.

A table of six or seven bikers across from us were being loud and joking but not obnoxious. One of them looked over at me and nodded. I nodded back.

"What are you riding?"

I look at him, confused. I'm trying to figure out what to eat and what my three kids are going to semi-eat so I can finish for them.

"What are you riding?" He repeats it. He's still smiling but it's beginning to fall.

Sometimes I'm an idiot. Heck, most times if I'm being honest. I point out to the parking lot at my Hyundai. "The red Hyundai," I say.

Now the smile is gone and he's puffed up. No one else at my table or his is noticing the exchange. I wonder if I could get past and out the door before he crushes me. This guy is huge. And not happy.

"You a jokester?"

I shake my head. I definitely don't feel like one.

Luckily, his wife/girlfriend/significant other notices when he gets out of his chair. She also probably sees the look on my face and takes pity.

"Sit down. What are you doing?" She has a hand on his wrist now, guiding him back into his seat.

He turns to her and they talk quietly. I see her shake her head and point at my three young children who almost lost their father before they could eat burgers and fries.

"He has his family with him," she says. "Where are they riding? Think. Leave the poor guy alone. He's trying to enjoy his lunch." She leans forward and mouths *sorry* to me.

I thank her and put my head down in the menu.

When their table leaves the guy stops in front of me. I haven't even gotten my burger yet. I'm too young to be beaten up in front of my kids.

"Sorry, man. Really sorry. Have a great day," he says. He slaps his meaty hand on my shoulder, nods, and leaves.

I find out when we're done he's already taken care of our check and the tip.

It ended up being a great day with my kids and a great story to tell over the years, like now.

The biker in the parking lot today gets his ticket, smiles and chats with the police officer for a few minutes like they're old buddies, and they both ride off.

I sip my coolatta and head to my Dodge Charger. Coincidentally… also red.

Friday October 18th

4110 NW Circle 326, Ocala FL at 7pm

Large hot chocolate with mint

Large sweet tea (wife)
The Bismark donut (wife)

On the way to a fantasy/horror convention in Tampa and we stopped at yet another gas station with a Dunkin inside. Before this month, I thought the only Dunkin spots inside gas stations were a small kiosk with a few donuts and maybe coffee if you were lucky, but I wouldn't be able to use my DD Perks card at the gas station register.

I need to pay more attention to the phone app when looking for a new Dunkin to visit, I guess.

My wife wanted a donut and asked for a vanilla creme filled.

"The Bismark?" Amber, who was helping us, asked.

My wife and I both looked confused.

"Not sure what that is," my wife said. "I just want the vanilla creme filled."

Amber smiled. "The Bismark. You got it."

I'd never heard it called anything but a vanilla creme filled. In fact, at every Dunkin I'd gone to it was clearly labeled as such. In this location there was no label in the rack where the vanilla creme filled/The Bismark was located.

Whatever you want to call it, Amber, is fine with my wife since it was still delicious.

Of course, I had to look it up.

According to an article I read on the Dunkin website from May 22nd 2019 titled "Boston Kreme vs. Bavarian Kreme vs. Bismark: What's the Difference?," it's called a Bismark, although Amber was very specific in calling it *The Bismark*.

A Bismark includes more dough, more filling and more topping because of its rectangular shape. See? Delicious. The article also says it's called a Long John down south.

Spitting crazy knowledge atcha in this book, too. You're welcome.

The location flows right from the Dunkin to the gas station side with a couple of tables for patrons to sit and enjoy their coffee and Bismark. The Bismark. Whatever. Delicious donut.

I'm also a big fan of mint, and went nuts the last time Dunkin had the Girl Scout flavors for their coffees. I could've done a month of Dunkin then because I was getting them like mad, and the mint was my favorite.

Having the mint flavor in hot chocolate is genius. I get lost in ordering hot or iced coffee all the time and never think about their ignored cousin, hot chocolate. No more. Especially if you are going to put some mint flavor in it.

If nothing else, so far, I'm finding a few new favorites and expanding my ordering for the future.

I imagine, come November, I'll be happily drinking hot chocolate with mint while munching on an apple fritter. And maybe seventy other combinations.

My wife is still talking about The Bismark as we get back into our car. She loved it but then again she says she is always a fan regardless of the fancy name you give it. I'm sure we'll be talking about this for days. Weeks. Months. It will be our little in-joke.

Or it won't and we'll immediately forget about it.

We've got another long weekend ahead of us with book signings and trying to locate another Dunkin each day, slipping away from the action in order to keep this book going.

Not to mention, keeping me and my wife happy with delicious drinks and donuts, regardless of what you name them.

Saturday October 19th

4404 West Grandy Boulevard, Tampa FL at 4:30pm

Medium hot coffee with almond milk

Half dozen donuts (me and wife) - Mine: Chocolate frosted with sprinkles, Double chocolate and French cruller

Large iced coffee with French Vanilla (wife)

We left the fantasy/horror convention after my last panel of the day and hit the nearest Dunkin. Luckily, Tampa has quite a few.

Unluckily, it was raining very heavily. Apparently the day before a vicious storm had run through the area nearby and did some damage to homes. We had no idea inside the hotel and doing our thing. We hopped between fat raindrops and got inside without being completely soaked.

The lovely girl behind the counter must've thought we were nuts. My wife and I have a tendency to put on a show when we're out in public, but not in an obnoxious way. We like to say nonsensical things to one another or toss out a volley of inside jokes to make each other laugh. Usually someone else around us gets caught in it.

"I'm going to have my usual," my wife says.

"No. I forbid it. You'll only have what I say you can have. Nothing."

"Now I'm going to order a donut, too," she says.

"There are rules you must follow."

My wife glances at me and then smiles at the lovely girl. "Ignore him. I do. I'm going to have three donuts. We're getting half a dozen."

"I said no… but I want anything with chocolate on or in it. Even near it."

At a supermarket, we can go on for ten minutes without missing a beat.

The bagger might ask if we need help with our groceries to the car.

"Why do you think I brought her?" I'll ask. Meantime she's the one paying because I'm clueless when it comes to shopping.

I can tell my wife is starting to see I can actually leave the house on my own each day and function in society. I have almost mastered using my DD Perks card and making decisions on my own.

My fear now is that she's going to use it against me.

"Can you run to the store and get me rice, beans and milk?" she'll ask as she's leaving for work. "So I don't have to stop on my way home tonight."

My stock answer used to be no. I'm busy writing today. I have things to do. I don't like to leave the house. I can't use a credit card correctly. I have no cash on me. I don't even know where the store is. I put my car keys down and can't find them. Locusts.

Now the cat's outta the bag.

I can leave the house and I can buy various items. I do know where my car keys are, too.

I'm no longer worried about locusts, either.

My only hope is for this book to sell so well I can hire someone to buy groceries for me so I never have to leave the house again. Maybe I can send my new assistant to Dunkin each morning for a large hot Britney Spears and an apple fritter, too.

The rain is coming in waves outside, slapping against the window. A few minutes later it slows down and the sun pops out, but the cycle continues in the hour we sit and relax and talk.

With the weather playing havoc there isn't anyone coming and going inside.

The inside of this Dunkin is big and bright, despite the clouds and rain. Lots of seating and windows. Very inviting.

Especially since it isn't raining inside the building, always a plus.

We eat our many delicious donuts and drink our drinks, chatting and relaxing. I've had to be on all day on writing and publishing panels, talking to an audience filled with my peers and/or wannabe authors. It is draining on me since I'm an introvert and being social destroys my psyche at times. I need a few minutes after each panel or conversation with someone to reset and talk myself into being a normal person.

I've done hundreds of conventions and book signings in the last thirty years, and yet… I freak out before each one. I sometimes have a panic attack. I hate crowds. Pushing through a hallway jammed with people is awful.

Relaxing in a Dunkin after a day where I've had to smile and talk with people? My reward. Getting to do it with my life is even sweeter. We get one another. We understand what the other goes through in their job and their strengths and weaknesses.

I just love this woman, who is going donut for donut with me while we watch the rain and chat. We have tonight to head back to the hotel and the con and figure out what we're having for dinner and then bed. Tomorrow I need to be up early for my last panel, see if I've sold any books, chat with new and old friends and fans, and then we hit the road for home.

But hopefully we'll hit another Dunkin on the way out of town.

...and then we don't, and it's really all because of me.

Please, let me explain.

Any time we're on the road my wife is usually driving. Ninety percent of the time. She'll argue it's more. I do not like to drive. I like to daydream and take naps, which is not good when you're behind the wheel. She sets the pace and all of that.

I could pretty much binge-drink coffee. Actually, at home I do. One cup after another. But on the road I leave it to her. If it was up to me we'd stop at every Dunkin sign we saw.

There are many times when my wife will ask me if I want a coffee. I always say yes. Then we go and get a cup of coffee at Dunkin.

But if she doesn't ask me I don't bring it up, unless we're about to start a trip. She knows I need coffee or I start to get a headache and grumpy. It's all a mental thing but she's seen it firsthand and I'm quite the jerk before that first sip smacks my brain and brings me to my happy place.

It certainly isn't her fault I don't drink a lot of coffee all day. We likely just left a Dunkin, where I had something to drink. No normal person would want to stop again two hours later, especially if we're almost to our destination.

As we do some shopping at the nearby mall and wait for the rain to end, I have the urge to get another cup of coffee. I won't be able to in the morning until we leave the convention.

I say nothing, because... not sure why. Another mystery about myself I need to explore, but not today.

Sunday October 20th

222 West Waters Avenue, Tampa FL at 10am

Large hot coffee with cream and sugar and hazelnut
Large iced coffee with French vanilla (wife)

I followed the directions as we left the convention to what I thought was a legitimate location. I guess it was. Inside the arena where the Tampa Bay Lightning played is legit, although we weren't going inside to check it out. Now… if there was a hockey game going this early in the morning, we would've gone. Plenty of parking close to the arena right now, too.

Luckily, there are a few locations in town, as we said yesterday.

Even after twenty days of doing this tour, I still want to automatically order the same thing every time. Creature of habit and all that.

I'm starting to get jealous of my wife, who doesn't have the rules I have. She can blissfully order the same drink each day and enjoy it. I have to find something new to eat or drink, and each day the large menu looks smaller and smaller as I check off another item.

Yes, I'm feeling whiny today. This is the second weekend of travel for us, although it isn't nearly as far away as last weekend. Still, we'd only been home a few days before hitting the road and hotel rooms again.

I'm also looking ahead to next weekend in Georgia for a few days as well. Another few days not sleeping in my own bed and surrounded by my stuff.

Am I complaining? Yes. Should I be complaining? Not really. I keep reminding myself that I'm wandering around, drinking great coffee and eating great donuts and sandwiches each day while the bulk of the population is going to a nine to five and working a job they might not like or definitely don't love.

I'm blessed.

So I need to stop whining about it.

Except that wouldn't really be me.

We find this location and make plans for the rest of the week, before we're headed to Georgia and another convention. This is a busy month for me, and I normally don't have three weekends in a row of traveling to book signings. Now I know why: it is draining.

Hopefully, by writing this down, I can remember not to book so many book signings with travel so close together. Unfortunately, it isn't up to me when promoters decide to book a show or signing. They are at the whim of a few factors most convention-goers don't even think about: when a hotel has an open spot to use the various banquet rooms, enough hotel rooms to be booked for that many guests, and when other signings or major events in the nearby area are going on.

I once drove twelve hours to a convention only to find out another book-signing event, this one at the nearby convention center, was going on the same weekend. A mile down the road. With some pretty big authors involved, a ton of media exposure, and free to everyone.

When I say we could've rolled a bowling ball down the aisles in the vendor room, I'm not exaggerating. Did the promoter know about the other, bigger event? I hope not. If he booked against something like that, thinking it would help his event, he was sadly mistaken.

Over the last thirty years I've done so many different types of book signings, and you never know what's going to work and what isn't. On paper some of them seem like a waste of time, and yet…

I once did a book signing with half a dozen other authors, all locals like myself, in a pool supply store. During a hurricane warning. In driving rain right on A1A, overlooking the churning ocean.

And I sold a lot of books that day, for whatever reason. The fact the store was busy, as if buying some chlorine for your pool during a hurricane was a top priority, still amazes me.

I've been to events that were talked about on the local news and radio, had some very big household name authors in attendance, and the years previous had been well-attended and every author came away having sold quite a few books. And then the bottom falls out for whatever reason, and either every person wandering through isn't buying books today or doesn't see anything that strikes their fancy, or the attendance is way, way down thanks to unknown factors.

You just never know, which is the fun and heartbreak of doing events.

It's something I struggle with, especially the costs involved upfront, like paying for a table to sell books, buying a bunch of books to hopefully sell, hotel rooms, food to eat, buying other books from other authors (supporting the cause, and I love books) and the other miscellaneous costs of being on the road and away from home.

Right now, though, as I think about all of this… I sip my coffee and watch the people coming in and out of Dunkin. None of them care about my whining, most of all my wife. It's time to head home with a quick detour to Gainesville to see our daughter and take her out to lunch.

I can sleep in my own bed tonight.

Monday October 21st

12740-200 Atlantic Boulevard, Jacksonville FL at 1pm

Large iced Signature Latte with caramel - Free!

The average elephant weighs twelve thousand pounds.

Another fact I hear on Dunkin Radio while waiting to order my drink. I've heard quite a few but this is the first one I commit to memory to share, and I have to cheat and write down the answer before I forget.

Don't get old. It's not fun.

I'd originally settled on an iced latte but Kaitlyn, who works here and is very friendly, suggested a flavor add. Caramel it is. I used another free beverage, too. I now have five left. Technically, the remaining five expire in November, but I should try to use them during this month.

I'm also guessing a couple more will pop up before the next ten days are done, too. Hard to believe this is three weeks of this already.

I am manic about checking the dates on the free beverages, too, even though I've committed them to memory. The absolute worst thing would be to miss using one and missing out on a free coffee. Can you imagine the heartbreak and loss?

My wife is worried, once the calendar turns to November, I'll go back to my old ways and never want to leave the house again.

Truth be told, I'm worried, too. While I'm having fun leaving the house and being out and about, I could easily slip back into my old ways.

A day like today is an especially big win for me because of the weekend of travel. It would be no big deal to stay home and get my house in order, figuratively and literally. I have a lot of laundry to do.

Nope. I'm out and mingling with anyone else who's around. Not that there is anyone else with me right now, which makes it hard.

It's probably after the lunch crowd and before the after school crowd, that weird twilight place each day. I remember it well from retail management: you could figure out which way your store went and when the crowds were coming, and get more work done at certain times. Usually. All it really took was a carload or a busload of people deciding they needed to shop right then, and your early afternoon when you thought you'd catch up on paperwork or resetting some endcaps was shot.

I am seated in a nice spot near the door, trying to write but actually watching the employees as they do their thing and take care of the lines that never stop forming in the drive-thru. As soon as I see less than three cars another one pulls up. It never ends, which is a good thing for Dunkin and the employees, since keeping busy makes the clock run faster.

Two guys, maybe in their late teens, walk in and look around. They're not looking for trouble but they are looking for someone. Since I'm the only person currently inside, they glance at one another and then me.

I decided to make this easy on them. I nod my head and make eye contact.

"That your car outside? The red one?"

I nod. "It is." Once again my red Dodge Charger has started a conversation. Truth be told, it was my wife's car first. When we met she had it, but when we bought her a brand spankin' new Ford Expedition, I inherited the Charger. I love the car, the way it drives and the looks, even if I know I look like an old man going through his midlife crisis.

The problem I have with driving a muscle car is the fact I'm a total poser. I know next to nothing about cars. I can barely change a flat tire, I kinda know how to check the oil, and I'm pretty sure I'm putting the right gas into it. Otherwise... I got nothing.

It doesn't stop these two from telling me everything I need to know about my own car, like they're reading from the user's manual. I wonder if they're goofing on me, too. They could easily slip in something like *how does the Jawa 396-A shake when you hit ninety?* And I'd smile and nod along.

When I slip in the reason I'm hanging out in a Dunkin sipping a latte and typing on my tablet, they seem nonplussed. "My mom wrote a couple of girly romance books a couple of years ago. Thought she was going to quit her job and become famous," one of them says. "She's still working and I don't think she writes anymore. She says it's a waste of her time until I go to college or something."

That makes me sad. It really does. This business is anything but a get-rich-quick scheme, and most writers aren't making a living at this. Heck, most aren't even making enough to pay their phone bill each month. I'm blessed because I make enough to keep doing it and my wife has a career so she can pay the bulk of the bills and I don't have to stress. Royalty payments are nice but they aren't steady.

Regardless of talent, someone who sits down to write usually has a passion for it. They write because they need to get it out of their system. It sounds like this kid's mom thought this passion she felt would be contagious to the outside world, and readers would flock to her book.

The greatest books I've ever written are hardly touched by most readers, who don't even know the books exist. It's more about marketing, promoting and sheer luck. Word of mouth has helped me sell more books than running ads, too. But you can't control it. You really can't control any of this. You just need to keep on writing and doing whatever needs to be done, even if it looks like it's pushing the needle half an inch at times.

"I hope your mom finds her passion to write again," I tell the kid.

He shrugs and then tells me more things about my car.

I sip my latte and nod at the appropriate times.

Another last fact for the day:

What's the hottest planet? Not Mercury. It's Venus, the second-closest to the sun. It's hotter, about nine hundred degrees, because it has an atmosphere.

Dropping more Dunkin Radio knowledge on ya.

Tuesday October 22nd

3411 Southwest Archer Road, Gainesville FL at 3:30pm

Apple spice donut

A very small location with a table and chairs outside and two chairs at the inside window. I chose the inside window because it was raining. A lot.

The drive-thru was constantly wrapped around the building and I'm guessing the bulk of their business is at the pickup window and not inside.

I was supposed to meet my daughter at this location. It's close to her apartment.

Her apartment. Even typing those words seems weird to me. She's my youngest. Nineteen years old and now in college.

Yes, in case I hadn't mentioned it again, I am old.

There are two older gentlemen seated outside in the rain, with the umbrella over the table not affording much protection from the rain. They're both getting wet but don't seem to notice or mind. They're talking about something obviously important. Not important enough for me to go outside and listen in, but important to them.

I wonder if they sat down before it started to rain and refuse to stop talking, or if it's been raining since they got here and they thumb their noses at a little rain and wind.

It's nice inside, which is where I'm staying.

I was hungry. It's a long ride to Gainesville from Jacksonville. Over an hour. Feels longer when you haven't eaten yet. So I get an apple spice donut and it hits the spot. It's another donut flavor I never think about, always going to the chocolate ones first.

I'm expanding what I eat and drink so far this month and wondering what other great things I've missed over the years by being so stubborn.

One of the old guys outside wipes rain from his forehead. His buddy is wearing a camouflage hat, which is soaking wet. They don't stop talking and laughing about something.

Still not going outside in the rain unless I have to, though.

As usual I'm a bit early and I keep checking the time. My daughter should be out of work by now, although you never know. What if she was asked to stay later, or she was in the middle of something? I'd hope she'd call or text and let me know she was running late.

The guy without the hat catches my eye. As I'm daydreaming I've been inadvertently staring at him. I do this a lot. Fix on a point in the distance and see right through it as the thoughts bombard me.

I look away but they've stopped talking. When I glance back up they're both staring at me.

It's uncomfortable because I didn't really do anything wrong or on purpose. Do I nod at them? Wave? Go out and say hi? No. Still raining out there.

The one with the wet hat says something and they both laugh, making me uncomfortable. I know it wasn't anything other than him probably saying I was eavesdropping or something simple, but now my mind is working. I'm a writer, after all.

Back to daydreaming, waiting for my daughter.

I don't even notice the two men have left until I look back over at the very empty, very wet seats.

After sitting for awhile with not much to look at besides the rain and the steady line of cars I make a bold decision. I text my daughter and tell her to meet me at the nearby Chinese buffet.

It works out perfectly.

Since she's just gotten out of work and ran home to take a shower, we end up arriving at the same time and enjoy a lot of food.

Conveniently, but not a setup at all, there is a Dunkin in the next shopping center. So after we eat we take a walk, which I do not suggest when you're old, it's super muggy now that the rain has stopped and the sun is about twenty feet off the ground and I'm old.

I think I mentioned the old part already, but you get the idea.

Old men don't like walking in sweltering heat.

7011 West Newberry Road, Gainesville FL at 5pm

2 Large cold brew coffees with caramel swirl

Both drinks aren't for me. I let my daughter choose our drink but go down the menu and point out every one I've already had this month.

While the list isn't exhausted, after three weeks of doing this, it is getting a bit narrower.

She is a big fan of cold brew, so that helps.

My daughter is now nineteen and in college. I'm amazed. Not that she's nineteen or that she went to college, just that it feels like yesterday she was born.

Which leads me to a story she's heard a thousand times already, but one I enjoy telling.

She was born in October of 2000 while I was still in New Jersey. Her mother was pregnant with her. Very pregnant, as they say.

It was decided this baby needed to come out as soon as possible, so we got in the car to drive into Red Bank and pop out this kid. From where we lived it was about a fifteen minute drive, the doctor knew we were coming, and ready or not a baby was coming.

Except for Jon Bon Jovi.

I knew Mister Bon Jovi, he of the golden singing voice and big home in the town we lived in, was having a shindig at his shanty. It was an invite-only event raising money for Presidential hopeful John Kerry. I was a big fan of his music, and the fact he was also a Jersey guy and he now lived a few miles from where I grew up was exciting.

Today I wasn't much of a fan because of the traffic snarl his event was creating. Katelynn's mother was *really* not impressed, especially since the labor pains were starting to irritate her.

We were stopped on a side street, thinking we could go around the blockades and police directing traffic to go in the opposite direction. A lot of other people had the same idea.

"Is that a cop up there? Do you know him?" She was driving, even though she was in labor. My hating to drive had started early. Before I could answer she got out of the car, waddled to the police officer, explained her situation, and we were waved past a line of really angry people. Maybe they thought we were going to the party. Maybe they thought I was a rock star. Maybe they were just mad we got to cut in front of them.

To this day, every time I go over the bridge into Red Bank when I'm back home, I remember how cool it was since we were the only car on the bridge. No one else was getting in or out of Red Bank coming in from there.

Then Katelynn was born. Nearly as exciting a story.

To this day, whenever she's in the car and a Bon Jovi song comes on, I tell her this is her heritage. She usually shrugs and silently hopes I stop saying it.

Side note: I worked in Red Bank for a few years selling footwear, and Jon and his wife would bring their daughter (who was maybe two at the time) in to get her a new pair of shoes. The first time this happened I was wandering around trying to look busy when he walked in, wearing sunglasses, and gave me a nod. I welcomed him and watched Jon go to the back of the store to join a woman and her daughter. It hit me seconds later who he was.

Like I said, I'm a big fan. I grew up on his music. I was in my mid-twenties at the time and my buddies George and Frank listened to everything Bon Jovi.

I was hoping one of his songs would come on the radio, since we were listening to a local rock station. I also wanted to say something to him. Thank him for the great music. Tell him about the many shows we've seen over the years. Say something to Jon Bon Jovi.

What did I say? Thanks for coming, as they left.

It's obviously haunted me twenty-five years later.

Anyhoo… I'm sitting with my daughter enjoying my cold brew and dreading having to go back in the thousand degree heat, taking in the air conditioning while I can.

My opening question is one I like to use to get your mind flowing, the creative juices moving around in your thoughts. The spark to ignite a wonderful back and forth.

What do you do?

Unfortunately, when posed to my daughter, she asks a dozen questions and is stumped immediately, trying to figure out the parameters of what I'm truly asking before she answers.

She is so my daughter, worried about everything and anything, even the smallest detail. For that I am sorry and I have failed. Katelynn has also inherited my sarcasm and wit, and for that I am not sorry.

"What defines me? I'm the daughter of millionaire author Armand Rosamilia," she says with a smile.

See? Sarcastic. I wish she could say that with a straight face. I mean, I am an author and it definitely feeds my ego when anyone asks any of my kids about their father and they can tell them I'm a full-time author. The millionaire part would be pretty cool, too. Not gonna lie.

Now she's worried about all the noise she's making with her ice in the cup and I have to explain to her no one will actually hear this interview, it will be written out in the book. Unless, of course, they hear the audiobook version, but there probably won't be ice noises in that version, either.

"Next question," Katelynn says, as if she's confident she can answer the next question without first giving me a dozen questions to define it.

"How's college so far?" I ask.

"It's pretty rough so far, as you can tell from a few weeks ago."

I nod. A few weeks ago was when she had her first freshman breakdown. I was surprised it took her about a month before she called me crying like she'd lost her favorite pet, wailing so hard I couldn't understand her at first.

Lots of *I can't do this, I want to go home, I don't like college, this is too hard, I'm lonely, I have no friends here, everything is too different…*

We'd been waiting for this phone call for awhile, and quite frankly I was impressed it took about four weeks to come.

I'm sure not all children who are tossed off to college the first time have these breakdowns, but I haven't talked to anyone yet who doesn't have their own story from either their time going off or when they sent a teenager off to college to fend for themselves in the semi-real world for the first time.

We'd helped secure and rent an apartment, paid for her classes, and gave her a bunch of items she'd need to live, but you can't do much more than that. It's the first time she's on her own. The first time she has no curfew. No set chores, no one telling her to clean her room. No one to make lunch or dinner for her. No one waking her in the morning to get to class.

"All of this is so foreign to me," she admits. "I just don't want to go to class. Not because I don't like it, but because there's no one telling me I have to."

It was overwhelming to her, which was expected. All part of growing up, gaining independence and freaking out like a teenager as a prelude to many freaking out moments as an adult.

Of course, she doesn't want to talk about her meltdown. Can't wait until she reads this.

She got a job, which definitely helped, too. A bit more independence, some money in her pocket and the ability to pay for some of her school costs, having gas in her car... more freedom to make the right and wrong choices. Again... all part of growing up.

Never mind it's making me feel old just thinking about it.

She has also inherited my self-deprecating humor, too. "I thought the Freshman Fifteen wasn't real," she says with a huge smile. "Oh, it is real. I'm on ten now."

I must look confused because she explains to me the idea that you'll gain fifteen pounds on average once you're in school your first year. I had no idea this was a thing. To me that's just a normal year gaining fifteen pounds. My goal is to live to be a hundred so I can weigh an even one thousand pounds.

"I'm getting used to school," Katelynn says with a shrug and a last sip of her drink. "Hopefully it will just get easier now that I'm working, making some friends and getting into the routine of classes and homework."

To switch the topic and make it a bit more light, I ask her to tell me something about her I don't know.

The deer in headlights look on her face makes me frown but then she laughs. "Uh… no. You're my dad."

I don't want her to tell me anything that will make me mad. "Tell me something that won't make me mad."

"I can't. I don't have one," she says. "Every story I can tell you will make you mad."

I'm hoping she's being sarcastic. Just more of that Rosamilia humor. She's never been in trouble. Never hung out with the wrong crowd (she's hung out with some pretty awful people, but they're selfish and rude but not criminals) and never got defiant about anything. Luckily she never wanted piercings or tattoos or dyed her hair pink and purple.

She's thinking of something to tell me that won't get me angry, which I appreciate. I finish my drink.

"I credit you with my Dunkin obsession," she says. "I have nearly as much as you do now."

I doubt that, but I know she has it a lot. It is another wonderful thing I've passed down to her. It almost makes up for the neurotic attitude and being scared of her own shadow at times thanks to me.

Almost.

We finish up and walk back through the hot, wet soup that is Florida heat after rain.

I'm proud of my daughter for making the necessary adjustments with college life. I'm proud of her for trying to figure it all out.

I make sure to give her a hug before we part ways and let her know how much I love her.

I also make sure to crank the air conditioning in my car when I get in, too.

Wednesday October 23rd

1310 Palm Coast Parkway, Palm Coast FL at 11am

Large hot black coffee

When I lived in the area I used to come to this location and sit in my car and write. I was broke and didn't have money to get something to drink every day, so I'd grab their wifi and work. Some days, if it was too hot, I'd go to the library and write.

This location was always busy and I was sad to learn it had caught fire in May 2016 and had been closed for eleven months before reopening.

The new building is pretty much the same concept as it was outside, although I really like what they've done inside. Lots of seating. A couple of high tables and an eight-seat table in the center of the room.

Even the display cases (this location also has Baskin Robbins) are updated and bright.

Judging by the heavy foot traffic as well as drive-thru line, I'd say this spot is even busier than I remember it. Even with two other Dunkin locations in town, it's still steady.

Lots of people are taking the time to sit and enjoy the space, too. Most of the seats are taken by a single person or a small group. Lots of conversations, some folks working on laptops, others on their phones. A few people enjoy a break from their daily routine.

I drank black coffee today.

Very rarely will I drink black coffee. I need something in it. Sugar and cream, usually. Flavored creamers is my new jam. I love having something in it to dilute the coffee taste.

Not that I hate the taste of coffee, I just prefer an enhancement to it. When I started drinking coffee in my late teens, I used so much milk and sugar you could barely taste the actual coffee. I slowly weaned myself off of so much milk and sugar, although I still prefer quite a bit. I am a fan of the Britney Spears, after all.

Growing up, my parents drank a lot of coffee. They still do. Can't start a day without it, and never even try to talk to my mother before her first sip. Same with me.

I started drinking coffee in high school when I needed to either stay up to study (which, let's be realistic, was very rare) or if I wanted to write my next epic novel that would putter out weeks later (this was when I mostly drank a lot of coffee).

Coffee became an addiction, something I needed each day. It became not only part of my routine but part of my life. It gives me great pleasure to have readers and fans who give me coffee and coffee mugs at events, because they know what a huge fan I am of it.

I was going to sit outside in the patio area but it was filled with customers enjoying the weather and the food and drink, so I took a spot at a small table so I could see everyone.

David Royall has been a friend for many years. He's a self-acknowledged bum but I suspect he's just retired. We met at a meetup for entrepreneurs and business people to meet and share ideas and have been friends ever since. Easily over eight years now. When I lived in the area we'd get together as often as possible, but now that I live in Jacksonville and do so much traveling, and he and his amazing wife Jill do a lot of traveling as well, these get togethers are few and far between, which is a bummer.

After David has a cup of coffee in hand and joins me at the table, we start our chat. He and I can talk for hours on any number of subjects. He's a few years older than me, has lived a vastly different life and sees things from his own unique angle. Our conversations sometimes take up a better part of an afternoon. He likes to say we're solving all the world's problems over a coffee or a beer.

I ask him what he does.

David pauses and I see the wheels turning. He has a great way of thinking through a question before opening his mouth. "If I didn't mention photography, then I'd be lying."

It's true. He's been taking pictures for a long time, and ever since I've known him, he's been upping his game with photos.

"I saw a meme online that said *it's not about perfection, it's about passion*. When I start to look at it that way, every photograph I take I see flaws in it. But I also really like the picture. I realize it's never going to be perfect, but it's what I love to do. The passion of taking that shot. That second in time."

I asked him when it really started for him, when the passion taking pictures took over.

"In the nineties I was working for the government. I traveled a lot." David smiles. "That was when I started running into Dunkin Donuts for the first time, too. I was going to some pretty nice places. I started carrying a little Kodak APS camera with me. It fit in my pocket, and that was my rule. It had to be small enough I could stick it in my pocket. I just started taking pictures everywhere I went. As soon as I got home I'd have to take it to the drugstore, wait a few days and get them back."

Yep, that's how us old people had to do it. None of this instant gratification on your phone. You had to pay per picture, too, so you made sure your shots counted. The old days.

"When digital photography came out, the game was over. I was hooked. Then I didn't have to deal with the drugstore anymore," David said.

Did he ever have a big camera setup?

"I did when I first got out of the Air Force. I had the camera with all of the interchangeable lenses. It was too bulky for my lifestyle. When the digital wave hit, I liked it. Big fan. You were able to do so much more with it, and it was all smaller. They could put more transistors on a chip and whatnot. Small cameras that were perfect to fit in my pocket. Now, with the iPhone, it further feeds my passion."

I ask if his shots are set up ahead of time or if it's more organic and in the moment, where he sees something and decides to pull out his phone and shoot.

David laughs. "What I just did with my donut is about as far as I'll go to set anything up." He'd taken a picture of his donut for social media, knowing I'd already done the same with my coffee. "Otherwise, I take the shot as I see something that catches my eye. I might manipulate it a bit to take some clutter out of it, but otherwise I shoot what I see. To me it's a documentary of what is happening around me. Capturing the moment for future use."

Future use?

David shrugs. "It started as taking pictures with the idea of writing a future memoir. I figured when I got old, which I am now, I could sit down and write my memoir. The pictures would be used in the book. If nothing else they'd be memory-joggers. It became habit-forming and addictive to keep taking pictures. I take at least one picture every day now, and it doesn't really matter what it is."

He's done a photo book, had his shots put onto pillows, and I look forward to his birthday and Christmas cards he makes each year.

"I went to a reunion of old friends a few weeks ago, people I grew up with. They were telling me I should be selling the pictures. Making a coffee table book of shots, things like that. Do a gallery showing. Thinking about it… that's not where my passion lies. I'm perfectly content sharing my pictures on Facebook."

It's a weird, slippery slope when you begin to monetize a passion. I realize not everything I write is because I'm one hundred percent committed or passionate about the project, but it needs to be done to pay the bills.

David nods in agreement. "My mother used to paint some really beautiful pictures. I used to take pictures of her paintings. One year I told her I wanted to make greeting cards out of some of her paintings. She had a fit. There was no way she'd let me do it. She said she'd never pick up another paintbrush if I did it. At the time I didn't understand what her problem was with it. I knew those greeting cards would sell really well. But, like you said, it was the thought of monetizing her passion. She didn't want to deal with that. Now I understand."

I ask about all of the travel David and Jill do all the time, and if it's given him so many great opportunities for pictures.

"Our last trip we were gone for thirty-seven days. Only two of them were planned. We had to be at the Albuquerque International Balloon Fiesta because we had reservations. We left Florida and headed west. Most mornings we woke up and had no idea where we'd spend that night. We'd just start going in a direction of our choosing, spur of the moment."

Are they taking their time each day and not spending it driving?

"Yes. We went diagonally across Nevada going from Vegas to Reno. There isn't much in-between except for stuff the military likes to blow up. We stopped in this little western town, maybe a few hundred people lived there. It was a perfect town, especially for the area. It broke up the seemingly bland trip through the middle of nowhere for us."

Where there other places you really wanted to see on this trip?

"Back when we first started talking about the trip, about a year before, I was talking to a friend of mine online. He'd just moved into a new house. I was joking with him about stopping by on the way to the Balloon Fiesta and seeing his new place in Nevada. It started off as a joke but he kept talking about it. The joke became a plan. So we knew we were going to stop in Reno to see his new house, too. Once we started planning the trip, or the few things we were actually going to plan, we needed to give him a set day and time we'd be there. He couldn't put his life on hold, waiting for us to get there. It was the second date we had to nail down."

What's next?

David shrugs and gives me a smile. "I've only been home about a week. This is the first time I've left the house except to get gas in the car. I feel like an astronaut returning home. I'm not sure how we're going to top this trip." His smile gets bigger. "But I know we will."

"I think it's time for us to have lunch," David said, reading my mind. "Where do you want to go?"

I chose the nearby European Village area, where I could get some Italian food while seated outside with David, finishing one of our many amazing conversations.

5290 East 100, Palm Coast, FL at 4:30pm

Medium sweet tea
2 jelly filled donuts

After catching up with world traveler David Royall at Dunkin and then lunch (I had a meatball sub, which I'd been craving for weeks) and stopped to see an old friend who runs a cigar shop, I hit the road north and toward home. But first… another Dunkin stop.

This location is one I used to either go inside and order or use the drive-thru with equal measure. Not sure why. I used to have a buddy who I wrote some books with who also lived in Palm Coast, and we'd spend a few Saturdays writing together. We'd stop here first to get our coffee and tea (he drank tea, not me) and then spend the day cranking out words.

The coffee would wake me up, put me in the mood to write, and we'd get a lot of writing and talking all day.

This Dunkin offers a few seats but they're all presently filled with high school-aged kids who likely wandered over after late study classes, afterschool sports or they just don't want to go home yet. Since the high school is a block or so away, I'm guessing this location can get busy when school lets out.

I didn't have a Dunkin or anywhere within walking distance when I went to high school. I had to walk to and from school if the weather wasn't too bad, and it was probably five miles. No, it wasn't uphill both ways, and I know I'm sounding like an old man again.

Back in my day…

I'm glad there wasn't a store on the way home, because I would've spent what little money I had on junk I didn't need. Of course, if I had a Dunkin on the way, it would be money well-spent. I also wouldn't have been so tired after walking home from high school, either.

Since it's a nice day out, I stand outside and wait for a table to open up. The kids are also out front, and they're fluttering from table to table, sharing the day's gossip, playing around and enjoying life.

I suddenly feel awkward and creepy. I'm standing against the wall sipping my sweet tea and shoving donuts in my mouth. I slink away but I feel great. I mean, it's a Wednesday afternoon and a lot of people are staring at the clock, waiting for their work day to be over.

It's days like this that remind me I need to get out more. See the places and people I used to see all the time. At times I forget I need to interact with other people besides my wife and online friends.

Getting out and going for a long drive while cranking my 80's hard rock music is needed at times, and even though I'm out and about each day, I have blinders on. I worry about getting from point A (my house) to point B (a Dunkin) and not enjoy the ride back and forth or the weather, the freedom and the music.

This drive is always fun because I used to live in Palm Coast and it allows me to see how the area has grown and changed since I've lived here.

Plus, when I leave to go home, I cruise north on A1A and turn the music up even louder.

Thursday October 24th

741 Cassat Avenue, Jacksonville FL at 11am

Pumpkin muffin

I know it's not the case, but I feel like I'm starting to run out of new things to try. Since I've so far resisted all pumpkin items but a drink in the beginning of the month, I decide it's time to dive back in.

Guess what? The pumpkin muffin is moist and not overpowering, which is the opposite of how I went into it. Pleasantly surprised. My buddy J.C. Walsh will be proud of me.

This is another location that doubles as a Baskin Robbins, too. The line for ice cream is six deep, while there's only two people in front of me for coffee. And pumpkin muffin.

I want ice cream, too, but I'm being good. I'm not sure if it would count as a purchase in writing this book, too… although I make the rules.

There is a gentleman seated directly across from me, so we're effectively staring at one another as we both eat muffins. It's my fault, since he was seated first.

We're acting like we don't notice the other person because it's weird being so close and facing one another. An empty table is between us.

I wonder if I need to move my seat, but we're currently the only two customers sitting inside so that would be a weird thing to do. Especially since I am such a sloppy eater and my goatee is packed with pumpkin muffin crumbs. If I stand too soon they'll go everywhere.

I'm so worried about this guy, who keeps glancing in my direction because I'm right in his line of sight, I can't concentrate on working on this book or anything else.

More pumpkin crumbs fall into my goatee and on my shirt.

I look at him but he's neat. He understands how to eat a muffin, unlike me.

We keep making accidental eye contact and then look away.

I imagine he's looking outside, behind me, and my excuse can be I'm checking out the menu again in case I want another muffin.

We get in another quick look and turn away again.

I wonder which of us would win in a staring contest. He's a little bit older than me and looks tough. One of those guys who doesn't need to look hard like he could break you in half because *he just can*. He exudes a confidence that says do not mess with me while I eat this muffin and sip this coffee.

Or maybe none of that is real. Maybe he's just a guy taking a break at Dunkin and enjoying his late morning coffee.

Maybe he's wondering why I keep looking at him.

Now I'm wondering why I keep looking at him.

As I'm thinking about looking at him I actually look at him and our eyes meet again.

I look away first.

We're still the only customers inside, even though the lines are moving but people are taking their items with them.

I try to concentrate on writing. Maybe if I get into the zone and my fingers start pecking away at the keyboard I'll forget about the guy and get some work done and…

He's looking at me. I know this because I look at him but then I look away. Again.

Why do I keep blinking first?

Is he doing it on purpose, getting some sick pleasure out of seeing me look away first?

I summon a strength deep within my body and soul.

I shall not be intimidated. I shall not look away.

He's sipping his coffee but looking at me as my eyes rise and meet his steely gaze.

No blinking. No surrender. This is a battle I shall win.

Now we're locked. He puts the coffee cup down without looking at it.

Neither of us look away. Neither of us blink.

He definitely knows what's happening, and he has risen to the challenge.

I put my coffee cup down, too. It seems like the proper way to win this event.

He's not blinking. I'm not blinking.

Long moments pass.

The door opens but I don't snap my head in that direction. It doesn't matter who's entered the building, because I am *laser focused.*

If need be, I will stay here all night. Is this a twenty-four hour Dunkin? I hope not. At some point I'll need to drink something. Maybe eat another pumpkin muffin.

This guy obviously has nothing to do today except relax in Dunkin. It might be getting closer to noon. It might be hours have passed and it will be dark soon. My wife will wonder where I am. She'll call me, breaking my concentration.

We keep staring.

I either imagine or really feel sweat beading on my forehead. My eyes are drying out by the second and now I fear I'll lose a contact lens, which will pop out and be lost in my muffin crumbs.

He seems as cool as a cucumber. As cool as the other side of the pillow. As cool as…

I blink.

At first I don't realize I do but the guy shakes his head and chuckles.

I've lost this epic struggle, a battle as old as time itself. At some point in the distant past, two cavemen sat in this very spot across from one another, on two boulders, and stared at one another.

He gets up and stretches, maybe to rub it in or maybe because he needs to stretch, takes his coffee cup and walks past me.

"You have a great day," he says and winks at me.

I can do nothing but laugh and tell him to have a great day, too.

Even in losing I feel like I won.

But mostly I feel like I lost.

Friday October 25th

1317 King Avenue East, Kingsland GA at 8:30am

Large hot dark roast coffee
plain bagel with strawberry cream cheese

Large iced coffee with French vanilla (wife)
plain bagel with strawberry cream cheese (wife)

Another weekend and another convention. We're on the road headed toward Dalton Georgia for Hallowcon. It will be my first time there and I'm one of the special guests.

But first a stop in Dunkin. Even though we're now in Georgia, this location is about thirty minutes from our house, closer than a lot of them in Jacksonville.

My goal was to save this stop in case I needed the closest one in the last few days, but the reality I needed coffee so badly this morning trumped everything else.

There's a fine line between waiting to have my first cup of coffee and being miserable not having my first coffee yet. My wife has figured out what my breaking point is and does her best to get me my coffee so I'm not a jerk until I get it.

The woman is a saint. She's also going to hurt me one day if I snap at her for not having coffee yet.

We usually stop at this location on the way north, especially when my wife has work in Atlanta and I take the ride with her. This might be the first time I've gone inside, though. The drive thru is usually really busy and parking in front of the Dunkin means you could be trapped with the way the drive thru lane snakes past it. We park next door at the gas station. My idea. My wife gives me a sigh because I'm an old man and I have to plan for things like this.

Or things that might happen but probably won't, like us getting trapped in a parking lot.

I notice, as we walk up to the doors, the line for the drive thru is only a couple of cars and anyone parked in front can easily drive away.

Inside we get in line with a bunch of other people. I always wonder where everyone is headed at this specific time of day. It's a Friday, so maybe a few of them decided to take off and have a long weekend. Maybe they're heading to work now, which is likely for a lot of them.

I realize I spend way too much of my time wondering what other people are doing instead of enjoying the moment.

My wife doesn't seem to worry about any of this, because she is a normal member of society. She's probably just happy to be off from work today, although I always wonder if these long road trips with me, so I can sell a few books, drive her nuts.

The plain bagel with strawberry cream cheese is perfect today. In all ways: it is thick but not too round, crunchy on the outside but soft and delicious when you bite into the bagel itself. The cream cheese is thick but not gushing out of the sides, and it has been toasted but not overdone, so it is warm but not hot. If you toast a bagel with cream cheese for too long, it begins to leak out on all sides.

This bagel is also fresh. I sometimes worry a bagel has been sitting in the bin for awhile. Maybe they pick a bagel that's small or really so thick the middle is more mush than fluff.

Yes, I think about these things. It's how my brain works. How I'm wired. I'd love to say it's because I'm a writer, but we all know it's just because I think like this.

People are coming and going and I don't even think about talking to anyone. I'm fascinated by this plain bagel. The only way it could be better was if it was a cinnamon raisin bagel.

I can't imagine a world in which I couldn't eat a bagel at least every three or four days. Ideally, each and every day. I love to put everything on a bagel instead of boring bread: burgers, tuna, cheesesteaks, pork roll, egg and cheese… if you can put it on a slice of bread, in a roll or even a pita, make mine with a bagel, please and thank you.

As we leave I glance at the line of cars in the drive thru. They're moving quickly, and if we'd parked in front of the building we could get into the car and drive away.

A glance at my wife tells me she's thinking the same thing. She gives me another pity-filled look, but

I wonder if it's for me or for her marrying an old man.

In the next several hours, on the way to the convention, I decided not to ask her. Some things are better left unsaid.

Saturday October 26th

300 Smith Industrial Boulevard, Dalton GA at 8:30am

2 sausage egg wraps

Fire roasted veggie burrito bowl (Jay)
glazed donut (Jay)

10 blueberry munchkins (wife)

We leave the convention hotel and go up the road three miles to this location. It's crazy how worried I was when I started to think up this book, thinking there'd be somewhere on this month's worth of trips where the Dunkin would be many, many miles away.
Not the case.
My wife decides to sleep in after the long day of driving last night followed by convention festivities. Lucky for me I know another one of the authors that has shown up this weekend, Jay Wilburn. Of course, I'm the one who told him about the convention to begin with. He had a table in the dealer's room, facing a blank dirty wall. It should be no problem

outselling him, as I'm one of the Special Guests and have a nice table in the main room between two ferns.

They're really not ferns but I keep calling them ferns and my wife keeps telling me what they really are. I forget what they are and so... to me they are ferns.

Since Jay is also a light sleeper when in a hotel room, I meet him early, before the con gets really rolling, and we slip out.

I try the sausage egg wraps because I haven't had them before. They are tasty and good for you, too? Of course, I could eat another dozen of them because I can't help myself. I stop at two. Jay seems to be enjoying his burrito bowl.

I've probably done a dozen or more book signings and conventions with Jay over the years. We've shared many tables and helped one another sell books. We've even co-written several books together, and I'm going to shamelessly plug them for you in three... two... one:

The Enemy Held Near is a haunted house novel set in Atlanta

Yard Full of Bones is a cosmic horror novel

The Hidden Truth is a transgressive fiction novel

End shameless plug and back to our exciting story.

I ask him what he does.

"I write down stories and try to get people to pay me for the stories." Jay has a very dry sense of humor so I'm not sure if he's trying to be funny, ironic or telling the truth.

He's also a full-time author and does a lot of ghostwriting. For those who aren't sure what that means (and it doesn't mean he writes a lot about ghosts or he channels the ghost's stories into books, which would be amazing) it means he writes books for other people and they put their names on it and make the money, but he gets paid to write it and sometimes it is for a large sum of money. Sometimes it is not, as well. It depends how good you are and who is interested in having you write their book for them, mostly self-help and memoir releases.

"It can also be freelance work. Doing blog posts for businesses. Web content. The About Me page. It can be as small as text that goes on their flyers like copywriting. It goes all the way up to a legitimate author paying someone else to write their book for them."

Jay will never reveal who he's actually written for, which will kill his ghostwriting career in seconds, but he can give me some generic ideas and such.

"The majority of the books I write are for business people. Someone who's had some success in business and might even be a public speaker. A self-help person. Oftentimes they are very clear and articulate about their business model, and how you improve your life and that sort of thing, but there's a difference between communicating something verbally and on paper. They're very good at explaining what they believe and why they believe it, but they struggle making it into a coherent chapter of a book. They tell me their thoughts and I take notes. My job is to make it seem like it was still in their voice but now it makes perfect sense on the page."

I imagine many of these people believe in the beginning they can write their own book because they are so articulate.

"Exactly. I feel like I am good at both things. I've had opportunities to speak and I've done well, and I can write. It had never occured to me that they are two different skill sets. When you think about it with these types of people it makes sense, too: in a live setting, on a stage or on a webinar or public event, they have the crowd feeding back to them. They can read the people and if something is striking a particular chord, they can dwell on it a bit and push the conversation in a new direction. If they're losing the crowd during a certain part they can change it to find a new, engaging way to keep them interested. When they sit down to write it out in book form, it feels dead. There's no back and forth to make it better. They also might be a great speaker but they struggle with grammar. Their spelling is off or they're leaving out words. Typing a thought is very different than speaking it. Especially someone who's used to thinking on their feet. Sometimes they'll give me notes or write something out and send it to me."

Is it a lot of actual interviews? Phone conversations?

"Yeah. I used to record an interview but found they usually went off on tangents and got sidetracked too much. Now I find it more useful to just take notes. I'm pretty good about writing down enough so i remember what they've said. While I'm doing it I can also draw arrows back to the topic, so even when they're going off into the weeds, so to speak, I can circle back around easily enough when I'm actually writing it. I can also then expand them on my own. I've written enough of these that I know what is missing from the conversation, or what needs to be explained in further detail."

I imagine you've done so many of these ghostwriting projects and you have the idea whcre it needs to go, you can guide the interview in such a way it makes sense and is easier for you to get to the proper sequences and write the book itself.

"I try not to make it mine. I'm pretty good about capturing voice. The first couple of interviews aren't necessarily about the outline for the book. It's for me to get a feel for what they want and how they want me to say it. I've written quite a few religious books, too, and preachers will have a certain rhythm when they speak. You might have a picture in your head of what that cadence is, but it's really different for each person. I have to figure out what their thing is and not what the stereotype is already. For instance, they might say three words in a row when making a point, and all three words might start with the same letter. If he's starting with *determination* he'll likely then go to *destination* and then *driven*. As examples off the top of my head. I pick up on the fact he's saying things in threes and they have a certain cadence and fit. He might not even know he's doing it. He's written enough sermons in his life. It's now also the way he talks in normal conversation. I realized, in order to make the book sound like him, I need to make sure I'm doing it on the page, too."

Do they notice it?

Jay nods. "When you do well capturing their voice, they comment about it. Some will tell me how weird it is to see their supposed words on a page, and it's in their voice, yet they didn't actually write the words. That's what you need to do if you want to do it well. I'm good at what I do. I'm sure it's an ego thing, but it's the truth. I'm very good at what I do."

I spend the next few minutes goofing on Jay and his ego, which is fine, because he jabs right back at me and my ego. This is why we've been friends for so long.

I ask him how long he's been ghostwriting.

Jay thinks about it. "I went full-time into writing in 2013. It was in 2015 I started doing some ghostwriting. It was a really slow build. I started going on the websites and started really low, because it's all reputation-based. When you first start you're nobody and you have to take garbage jobs. For garbage pay. The hope is you do really well and they give you a great rating, which lets you move up the ladder to better jobs. Eventually I built it up and had hundreds of five-star reviews. People were coming back to me with future jobs, so I was able to pick and choose jobs I wanted to do. And that isn't just for books. I was doing blog posts, political speeches, short stories, web content, every genre of fiction and nonfiction. Romance fiction books were probably the most common followed by nonfiction self-help and business books. I don't do as much fiction as I used to now. It's mostly nonfiction for me."

Was that on purpose?

"Yes. It's a different kind of writing than what I do, so I'm not using the same pathways in my brain. Writing mostly nonfiction isn't making me tired and it allows me to go back and write my own fiction."

How did you even get into ghostwriting and aware it was a way to make money writing?

"I got into ghostwriting on purpose. I didn't want to go back to the day job. At point money was a little thin. Writing money is always sporadic. I had months where I made more than I did as a teacher, but that wasn't too common. It was very lean. Rent comes due the same time every month whether you've had a good or bad writing month. I needed to fill in the bad months. I knew ghostwriting was going to be a way to pay the bills and allow me to keep writing the projects I wanted to write as well."

What percent of your writing is your own as opposed to ghostwriting?

"If you go by word count it's only about ten or fifteen percent of my writing is actual ghostwriting. I'm now getting paid a decent rate, so I can pick and choose the projects I want to ghostwrite. I stay busy with them. Once you're doing one of those books, you're doing a chapter at a time. I'll have a couple of quick conversations with the client and do some of the writing one day. Then the ball is back in their court as far as when we can get to the next chapter. My turnaround is fairly quick, so I can do the interview with the client and write the chapter all in the next twenty-four hours. It takes them a lot longer to get back to me to either change something or move on to the next chapter. The breaks in between give me time to work on my own writing."

Do you think you'll ever get to the point where you stop doing ghostwriting?

"Yes." Jay pauses. "Because it's easy money for me… not every person can do what I can do easily… for whatever reason this is easy for me. I have many clients who come back for the second or third time to work with me. They pay well and pay on-time. It's hard to say no to that money." He's lost in thought again. "But if there was a certain amount I was making with my own writing, and it was as steady as writing money gets, and I could justify it in my mind… then I'd walk away from ghostwriting."

Would he miss it?

He nods. "I enjoy ghostwriting. The challenge of it. The ease of it at times. Interesting subjects I get to learn and write about. There are many factors, but in the end… I need to write what I want to write and make money to support my family."

We finish up and head back to the convention. Hopefully today will be the day we both sell a lot of books.

Unfortunately for me, Jay sells a lot more books than I do. Maybe it's another step in the direction to quit ghostwriting for Jay and start to write only his own books.

Sunday October 27th

675 Highway 53 East, Calhoun, GA at 8:30am

Medium hot coffee with cream and sugar
Sausage, egg and cheese croissant

chicken, bacon and cheese croissant (wife)
Large frozen chocolate (wife)

On our way home from another weekend of signing books and sleeping in hotel rooms. Yes, I shouldn't complain. Yes, I still do.

A couple walks in and goes right to the pickup counter and grabs their order, which is fascinating to me.

Not so much to my wife, who is way more in tune with technology.

"They used the On-The-Go mobile ordering," she says. I mean, not in those exact words like a commercial, where she then conveniently holds up my DD Perks card and smiles at the camera. But you get the idea.

"There's no one here right now. It isn't like the line is ten deep," I say.

"How do they know? Maybe they ordered from home and knew it would be ready by the time they arrived."

True. "I've never had to wait too long in a Dunkin. Plus, it gives me time to figure out what I'm eating or drinking."

My wife knows me too well. "You order the same thing every time: hot coffee light and sweet and a cinnamon raisin bagel with cream cheese."

"Not always," I lie.

She gives me the look to let me know she knows I'm lying.

I am a creature of habit. "I'm doing good with change this month."

She doesn't seem impressed. "Wait until November. Let me see what you order then."

My wife knows me better than I know me.

I will most likely order a large hot coffee, light and sweet, and a cinnamon raisin bagel with cream cheese. Creature of habit and all that.

I pull out my phone and check the Dunkin app. "It says I can get special things if I use the app. Two for five bucks on the bagels. Stuff like that."

"Don't you use your app every day?" she asks.

I shake my head. "I use the plastic card in my wallet."

She grins and I know she's calling me old man in her head. "Just use your phone."

"I use my phone when I have a free beverage coming." I say it a bit too defensively. I know it. She definitely knows it. "I let them scan it."

"Which you can do for every order and not have to use your card," she says. "Your card is getting beat up and chipped. Use your phone."

I shrug because I'm not going to use my phone except to get my free coffee. I like my beat up, chipped card.

We've got a long drive ahead that neither of us is looking forward to. If I'm being honest, the convention was a bust as far as book sales were concerned. Lots of people came to my table but they were more interested in telling me about the book they'll someday write, or asking me publishing questions. Only a few actually looked at the books on the table, and it was usually in passing.

Ahh, the fun of a book signing. You might sell a hundred books in an afternoon. Usually you sell way less than that. Sometimes you sell nothing at the event, but readers take your bookmarks, swag and business cards and buy a book online at a later date. You just never know.

I watch a few other customers in and out, but it seems like this part of Georgia wakes up a bit later than normal. Not too many cars in the drive thru, either. One or two at a time.

As we leave I feel good about the weekend. Not about sales but about networking with other authors, getting to hang out with Jay Wilburn and my wife, and being able to live my dream.

Now I just need to figure out how to sell more books. Easy enough… right?

This will be my last Dunkin visit out of Florida as far as I can tell.

Not forever. There will be many book signings in my future, and many will be out of state.

For now... we head home after another long weekend.

Monday October 28th

13627 Beach Boulevard, Jacksonville FL at 1pm

Everything bagel with cream cheese
Medium hot chocolate with caramel swirl

Today I had a few errands to run and decided to just drive in a random direction and see if I could find a Dunkin I hadn't been to yet.

I found this one.

Decent amount of room inside with several tables and chairs as well as a set of comfy chairs. When I arrive a guy seated at one of the two outside tables grins at me. "Maiden, dude. Way cool."

I'd been blasting music as I drove up in my red Dodge Charger. I love that car, even if it turns heads but people see me driving it. I wonder how many people half my age think I'm going through a midlife crisis.

Plus, I think I look cool driving with the windows down blasting *Run To The Hills*.

Not like the old man I obviously am.

Inside, two teenage boys are playing cards. Actual cards. Not Magic the Gathering or Yu-Ghi-Oh or whatever other newfangled card game these crazy kids play these days.

I wonder if they forgot their Cards Against Humanity and someone my age left a pack of playing cards on the table.

I settle in with my bagel and hot chocolate to write when I see a woman at the counter, waiting for her order, smiling at me.

I smile back.

She's pointing at my table. I wonder if I spilled something or she's laughing at the mess I always make.

It's the bookmarks.

"Is that you?"

I'm confused, which is very common. "Is what me?"

She puts a finger on the bookmark. "I'm following you on Twitter. I see these every day." She says the hashtag aloud. "I love this. Has it been fun? Are you getting good stories?"

I am. The fact someone in person is telling me they're following along is amazing, and the chance of running into her at a Dunkin is equally amazing.

I'd stopped posting where I'd be on the website when it got to the point where I had no clue where I was going the next day, or even as I grabbed my car keys.

"How did you know I was here?" I asked.

She shook her head. "Oh, I didn't. I just stopped on my way home for a cup of coffee. Your daily posts got me excited for Dunkin again."

Amazing. "Sit and tell me a story," I say.

She looks like a deer in headlights.

I smile and push out the chair across from me with my foot. Like in a movie. "Please... I'm Armand. Tell me what you do."

"I'm not very interesting," she says and her coffee is ready. She isn't leaving, though, which is a good sign. "I have nothing to say."

And then she does.

After some more small talk and her asking a few questions about me as a writer and how I make a living doing it, she gets comfortable across from me.

"I'm a bookkeeper in my son's body shop. See? Told you it wasn't much of a story," she says, her tone apologetic.

"How long have you been working there?"

"Five years. It used to be my husband's body shop." She sips her coffee. "That's it."

I doubt that.

"Twice a week I go in, sit at my desk, and pay all his bills and call people and make sure they're paying him on-time."

"That sounds like more than just bookkeeping," I say.

"Back in the day, before my husband sold it to me, I did it all," she says and takes another sip. "I used to change the oil and rotate tires, too. I can run circles around anyone when it comes to an engine."

I'm positive she can run circles around me when it comes to cars.

"Wait... you said something interesting."

She shakes her head as if I'm wrong.

I nod because I'm right. "Your husband sold you the business."

Now she takes another sip and I can see the wheels turning. She's wondering if she should say anymore. I don't want to push her, but I also want a good story. I'm selfish that way.

"You don't have to use my real name. Right?"

"Of course not," I say. "You don't have to give me any details unless you want it in the book, like the name of the body shop."

"My husband was an awful mechanic. The body shop was originally a garage he inherited from his father, and his grandfather had started it back when the area wasn't built up. It was on a dirt road. You could smell nothing but oil and the ocean, my husband used to say." She's animated now and begins using her hands to accentuate her words.

I sit back so I'm not struck in her enthusiasm and knocked out cold.

"When he took over the business because his dad was too old, he slowly converted it into a body shop. He wasn't great at fixing cars but at least he was better at it than fixing an engine. He could knock out a dent or paint a panel well enough."

I took a sip of my hot chocolate.

"He also got less complaints about it, too. We met when we were still in high school, and got married a week after we both graduated." She grins. "Young love is stupid."

I laugh at her remark.

"When I could, I helped out. He'd worked there all through high school. He never had any ambition to go away to college. Wasn't into sports." She grins. "He was head over heels in love with me, though. His daddy taught me how to change the oil one day because I was always hanging around, waiting for my boyfriend to get off work. I took to it. Before long, I was doing a lot of the work and his old man started to pay me."

I ask if that created friction between her and her future husband.

"Heck yes, it did. I was better than he ever was, and he'd been doing it since he needed a step stool to look in an engine. I was much faster, too, and after a few months customers started to ask for me to work on their car. Then we got married and he didn't want me to work anymore. He was going to take care of me."

I cautiously ask if it was more his ego than anything else.

She nods. "He swore it was because a woman is supposed to be home raising a family. He wanted kids. Lots of them. Boys who could take over the garage when he passed, that kinda thing. So… I got pregnant with my son."

I let her sip her coffee and look out the window for a couple of minutes. I fear she'll decide she's had enough of this reminiscing and run out, and I won't try to stop her.

She turns back to me and asks a few questions about me: more about being a writer, about my kids, about my wife, about how much coffee I'll drink this month. Since I enjoy talking about myself, I talk and talk, before easing us back into the interview.

I ask what happened to the business, figuring it was a generic enough question to start again.

"He did well for a few years. I stayed home and raised our son until he was old enough to start going to school all day. Then I went back to work, but he would only let me do the books and all that. He'd really screwed them up at one point and we owed the government a bunch of money." She smiles. 'Like a Springsteen song. You posted onc the other day on Twitter. I remember that but not which song."

I can't for the life of me remember what song it was, although I cheat later and look it up: *Darkness On The Edge Of Town*.

"I cleaned it all up for him. By then he'd started doing more body work, and did more work like that. We tried for more kids but it didn't take. Our son grew older and was using a step stool to get into the engines by that time, too."

I ask how skilled he was.

She is smiling again. "Somewhere between me and my old man. Let's just leave it at that. When he was ten." Now she's laughing. "By the time he was in high school he was working in the garage, and started to even work on changing oil and doing non-body work for his dad."

Her smile drops. "As soon as our son had graduated, he moved out with his girlfriend. Got a place right around the corner from the garage. By then this area was being built up. Lots of new roads and businesses. Developments and houses. The shop got really busy and our son went to work full-time with his dad. I got divorced from him. I couldn't take it anymore. We were two different people, and I knew he hated me being around the garage. That was his space and whenever I was there he felt put out. I'm not sure why. Maybe the ego thing."

I let her sit and drink her coffee for another minute in silence.

"My son really turned things around. My ex-husband was losing money left and right. Good with his hands but not with his brain. If it weren't for our son taking over and me doing the books, it would be long gone"

She'd mentioned she was the owner, or had been at some point. I gently coaxed her to tell me the story.

Now she's grinning again. "My ex decided it was time to get out. He'd met a woman a few years older than he was. I guess he thought he'd live off her money or something. They wanted to run off to Vegas and get married and live, I guess. She wasn't as dumb as he thought she was, though. She made him sell the garage, but since my son didn't have all the money, I bought it. Used the money I'd been saving the last few years, when I knew we were heading for a divorce. Got a small loan from the bank. Two years ago my son bought it out from under me. Like I said, he's doing great. If you need an oil change or something, I'll give you the name and address… but maybe not for your book."

It's obvious she's itching to get going so I thank her for her time and tell her to keep an eye out for the book.

She's quite happy. "Thanks for letting an old lady prattle on and on. It's nice to talk to someone different sometimes. I'll keep following along on your Twitter, and when the book comes out I'll be first in line to buy a copy."

I promise to message her when it does come out and meet her right back here with a signed copy and we can grab a couple of coffees and catch up.

Tuesday October 29th

7440 US 1, Suite 100, St. Augustine FL at 11am

Large iced coffee with cream, sugar and coconut power breakfast sandwich

I now have seven free drinks coming to me thanks to a Dunkin a day, but I keep forgetting to use them. In the next two days I'll need to get one or two in. November is going to be pushing myself to still leave the house even though this book will be technically finished, although there will be plenty to still write.

A few free coffees will motivate me to leave and go to a Dunkin and keep writing. I'm really enjoying this month of being out in the real world. Last night my wife told me it showed in my demeanor and interactions with her and others and that was a good thing.

I know she's right.

Maybe I'll have to do a last chapter, right before the book is ready to go to the printer, to update everyone whether or not I went back to my old ways of being a hermit.

It might also force me to get out of the house and my comfort zone.

I've been to this location before. In fact, I've been inside this location, too. No drive-thru quick stop for me. My wife and I came soon after it opened, and I happened to be wearing one of my zombie shirts.

The manager was very interested in my shirt, and she talked about zombie books. That was great, because when people want to talk to me about zombies it's usually about *The Walking Dead* or a movie they've seen. Hardly ever about books.

She was an avid reader of zombie literature, and we started to compare notes. I never know when I should slip in the fact I'm also a writer of zombie books, but I remember I did it smoothly and didn't feel like a jerk afterwards.

I always have to ask my wife if I overdid it or talked about myself too much.

This particular interaction seemed to be perfect, and the woman loved the fact she was meeting an author. She made my coffee (I'm sure it was a large hot Britney Spears) and food (cinnamon raisin bagel with cream cheese) and asked a bunch of questions about the writing process and who I knew that she'd read.

I remember the best part was that she didn't just know the typical writers like Stephen King or James Patterson. She knew the independent writers, which I am a proud part of, and named a few I was actually friendly with.

The conversation was great and she wrote my name down as well as the title of my zombie series

(*Dying Days* for those playing at home) and I left feeling great.

Today I also feel great. Bright sunny day. Driving with the windows down blasting my music. Living the dream.

The employees are all very friendly here, with big smiles and acting like they genuinely care what I want. When I order an iced coffee and stumble over what flavor to add, the cheery woman suggests coconut with cream and sugar. I accept.

I wish this location wasn't so far away from my house. It might be the perfect one to sit and write each day. Maybe I'll come back once or twice a month and get some work done.

I sit near the door, which is my spot now. Facing the menu and customers in line. I try to give a smile to anyone leaving Dunkin, even if I know I won't be doing too many more interviews, as the month is coming to an end quickly.

After yesterday's interaction with a customer, I make sure to keep the bookmarks I've made at the edge of the table so anyone can see them coming or going. While I've really only been leaving them each day after I go, I'm now wondering if i missed a big opportunity by not showing them off more and letting people actually see them as they pass.

Another learning opportunity and possibly another missed one, too.

A trio of women are seated nearby, and I can't help but eavesdrop. It isn't like they're whispering. One of them is so loud as she talks the employees keep glancing over at her, as if she's yelling at someone. I guess her friends are used to her being so loud because they don't flinch or look uncomfortable.

Loud Talker also uses her arms as she speaks, threatening to wipe out the trio's coffee cups.

Now I see her friends might not mind how loud she is, but they do mind if she takes out their drinks. In tandem they both grab their cup, take a sip, but don't put them back on the table.

I'm not even sure what Loud Talker is regaling them about, either. She keeps stopping her story and going back to a previous place in it. Something about being on vacation with her husband and something funny happened while they were on the beach... maybe. She goes back to before they left, when he couldn't find his t-shirts he bought specifically for vacation, and she's laughing loudly as she's trying to tell her friends. They are giving her smiles but they also seem confused.

Suddenly we're back on the beach and a hunk of a man, half her age and with muscles on muscles if she can be believed, is checking her out. Blatantly staring and flirting with her.

I'm more interested in her two friends and their reactions, which are clearly disbelieving. They keep glancing at one another. Loud Talker is oblivious, now going back to her husband and how jealous he can be whenever men stare at her. Then we're back on the beach and the hunk walks by and nods at her. They exchange a knowing glance.

Her friends try to change the subject, asking about how the weather was and where they stayed, but Loud Talker isn't done with her story. She's going on and on about the lingering look and how, if her husband saw it, he'd say something to the hunk.

One of her friends smiles. "Jerry would confront the man? He doesn't strike me as the type."

Loud Talker is newly revitalized, and now goes into a completely different story about the time in college when Jerry (not his real name, although I'm not sure why I'm protecting anyone) fought off three potential boyfriends for Loud Talker after class. Apparently, she was quite the catch, even many years ago in college.

I imagine her friends have had to sit and listen to Loud Talker many, many times. She won't let them get a word in, so they give each other knowing looks and sip their coffee while she talks so everyone in and out can hear.

It's hard for me to write because she is getting louder as she switches stories to a Christmas party where Tough Guy Jerry came to her defense again and threatened Loud Talker's coworker who made a pass at her.

The woman has to ask again, and I can see her look clearly: she doesn't believe Loud Talker. "Jerry did that?"

Her friend doesn't believe it, either.

Loud Talker pauses, coming up for air. It's all the time her friends need to firmly change the subject about their kids. They begin talking fast, as if to stop speaking would give Loud Talker an in to start telling another story about her husband fighting yet another man that wants to steal her away.

They aren't nearly as loud and I can get back to writing. Except I don't want to. I'm waiting to see if they can successfully shut Loud Talker out.

Alas... they cannot.

Loud Talker has no kids, although at first I think she does because she keeps mentioning her babies. I realize she has dogs. Her fur babies. While the other two are discussing their human children in class and an upcoming trip they'll be taking, Loud Talker is describing the funny things her puppies can do. Not nearly the same thing, and a real disconnect for Loud Talker, in my opinion.

Another ten minutes passes with Loud Talker successfully taking back the conversation and talking about a brand new subject: another upcoming trip her and Tough Guy Jerry will be taking to Hawaii.

Her friends give another look and both stand at the same time. Hugs all around. Quick goodbyes before they both hit the door.

Loud Talker looks around, still seated. When we make eye contact I look away and casually pull the bookmarks back across the table toward me.

I fear, if I interviewed her, my batteries in the recorder would run out, and you'd be reading a hundred thousand words about her and her wonderful life.

She leaves and I see a couple of other customers who'd been at the other end of the room start to smile and talk. Luckily they are talking much quieter than Loud Talker is capable of.

After twenty minutes of silence and writing, I start to miss her.

Wednesday October 30th

5150 University Boulevard West, Jacksonville FL at 11am

10 chocolate Munchkins

This is a location I've never been to, not even to use the drive-thru.

Despite having a lot of tables and chairs to sit at, I can't find an open one. Not even to sit with anyone else. Every seat is filled, and everyone seems like they're in no hurry to leave.

I've never had this happen and I have no idea how to react.

I stand, holding my box of Munchkins, and say nothing.

No one is going to leave. Ever. At closing, the employees will wave goodbye and tell everyone to have a good night, and shut off the lights and lock the door behind them.

The people will still be drinking coffee and talking.

I will be out of Munchkins by then.

Do I go back to my car and wait until someone leaves? Is there a reservation I need to be added to? *I'd like table three at noon for one. Name? Arcola.*

Story time while I wait for a seat: when I was growing up, I'm talking about my formative late teenage years, I'd go to lunch or dinner with my buddies. We'd go to the chain restaurants in town and never had a ton of money, being kids, but sometimes we'd go to the fancier chain places. Ones where you didn't get in line to order your food and find an empty table. Places with an actual hostess.

I would always try to get to the hostess first and leave my name. Try using my real name and see the blank looks you'll get when they try to spell it out. They never get it right. Ever.

So I began using a fake name for fun, so when they called it out my friends and I could get a cheap laugh. Nothing dirty. Nothing anyone would know except if you were about our age.

I'd use Chachi Arcola. As in... Joanie Loves Chachi. As in... if you're not nearing your fifties you're now scratching your head. Google it. You'll see what I'm talking about. Scott Baio was Charles "Chachi" Arcola. He first appeared on an episode of *Happy Days* as the cousin of Fonzie. Trust me and look it all up.

The grins I'd get from people waiting to be called for an open table was always more fun than the meal itself. It was also cheaper, and I do love a cheap joke.

It got to the point where my closest friends would let me put my name down because they knew what I was going to do, and it never failed to make us laugh. Even then, younger people who tried to read it, having no clue it was fake, didn't get it.

But we got it and it made us laugh uncontrollably as we were shown to our seats. You always remember the small things that get you through the awkward years.

I'm not sure if I've tried it in my (supposed) adult life. I feel like I tried to do it once when I'd first started dating my wife. I'm sure she thought I was an idiot.

Now I can't wait to try it again and see who gets the joke.

And if my wife will shake her head and pity me as usual.

While I'm stuffing Munchkins in my mouth and thinking about the good old days, a couple of people have gotten up and left, but new people have quickly filled those seats.

I feel like I'm never going to be able to sit down. Ever again.

Everyone is having such a great time and I feel left out.

It's like my teenage years all over again.

Munchkins done, I decide it's time to leave.

So I head out.

Arcola is leaving the building.

719 Atlantic Boulevard, Atlantic Beach, FL at 1pm

Large hot coffee with cream, sugar and French vanilla - free!

Frankenstein monster creme filled donut

I decided it was too nice of a day out to rush back home, so I took a quick ride and headed toward Jacksonville Beach, knowing this Dunkin was still waiting for me.

This is the location I try to remind my wife about whenever we're in Jax Beach for dinner. After a huge Italian meal at one of our favorite spots, we head home.

And at some point, if I remember to time it right, I give the very subtle sign.

"Hey, can we stop for coffee?"

See... subtle.

I'm alone inside so I take the best seat in the place, near the door so I can see everyone. If anyone comes inside. The drive-thru is steady as usual. I've never been inside before even though I've frequented this location at least a dozen times.

The employees are happy, and the one who helps me select my items is joking around with me and makes sure my coffee with French vanilla is perfect before I walk away. I believe his name is Mario.

One regret writing this book so far is not getting more of the employee names that have helped me along the way. I decided early in the writing not to bother them while they worked or act creepy.

I act creepy, not them.

There are even seats available, which feels like a bonus today. Unlike yesterday.

My wife sees the post I've put up on social media and now she's commenting on Facebook she wants a Frankenstein monster donut and asks about the filling. She's not a fan of the custardy filling so she passes, but I do my due diligence and ask if she wants anything else.

She passes. It's a much better option than me having to choose a donut for her. I am awful at doing it, and it's because I over-think it every time.

I know she likes chocolate. I like chocolate. It should be easy. Right?

Nope. Not when you second-guess and swear she's a bigger fan of the vanilla-filled donut.

Wait... now I think she is a fan of that one, too.

Ugh. Can my life get any harder?

Oh, wait... she didn't want a donut.

Now I'm second-guessing getting her one anyway. Maybe she's giving me mixed signals?

Nah. If my wife wants a donut she's going to tell me she wants a donut. That's why this relationship works. She doesn't beat around the bush because I'm horrible at reading Beating Around The Bush Signals.

Fingers crossed.

The employees are joking around about something and having fun, even as they're filling coffee cups and boxes of donuts for the drive thru crowd. This is definitely a team that enjoys working together, or they're amazingly good at faking it.

It hits me this is the end of this tour. Tomorrow is the last day for this book. Obviously not the last day to eat Dunkin but I won't be doing this every day.

I use one of my free beverages and hope to remember to use another tomorrow. It will still give me five left to use in November, meaning I'll be stopping at a Dunkin every few days to use them. Win-win.

Customers are coming and going but no one looks at me. So far it's moms with young children, the kids getting a Halloween donut and mom getting her iced coffee.

Three of them in a row, in fact.

The last mom has two young girls and I watch as the youngest keeps trying to stand on her chair. Mom is playing on her phone and waving her hand absently to tell her to sit, not really paying attention.

You can see where this is going. Amiright?

The kid slips but doesn't actually fall hard, but she has that stunned look on her face all kids get: am I fine, or do I start screaming now?

Mom waves her hand again,

Daughter begins to scream for attention.

Finally, the mom puts down her phone and looks at the girl like she's someone else's kid for a second before getting up and asking what happened.

"She was standing on the chair and she fell and hit her head," the other girl says, even though her sister did not hit her head.

Now the one who fell is touching the top of her head and crying even louder.

The mom looks over at me but it's more for me to mind my own business than a *sorry my kid is screaming because I was too busy looking at cat memes* kinda glance.

A promise of another donut and the little girl is suddenly fine and stops touching random spots on her head, while her sister pouts and I wonder if she'll fall off her chair next for attention and another donut.

Mom apparently doesn't like me glancing over there as I type. Maybe she thinks I'm recording the sordid affair, or she actually feels guilty about her daughter getting hurt. She tells both girls they have to go, sweeps everything off the table, and drags them to the door.

"But my donut..." I think the girl is about to hit the waterworks again, but her mom smiles and promises she'll go through the drive thru and get them both another donut.

Of course, I watch her get in her mini-van. She glances back at the building but she can't see me because I'm in stealth mode. Ok, I'm slumped down and against the wall now. Like I'm invisible and poof! Disappeared.

I watch the mini-van go around the building but when I stand and look at the drive thru window, I see her pass it.

No donuts for the girls. I hope mom doesn't text and drive, but I have a feeling her phone is vitally important to her at all times.

Thursday October 31st

7171 Phillips Highway, Jacksonville FL at 11am

Large cold brew Britney Spears - free!
pumpkin donut

As I get out of my car I hear someone talking to me. I turn to see an employee, standing near her car, admiring my ride.

"I love that color," she says with a smile. "And the car."

I'm also partial to my red Dodge Charger. Getting out everyday and driving around blasting music has really helped to clear my head and get better focus on the important things.

Like me leaving the house and not being moody.

"Any problems with it?" she asks.

We get into a quick conversation about cars but it's obvious she knows way more about it than I do. I bluff my way through a couple of things before heading inside. I know if I talk too long about stuff I don't know about, she'll figure out what an idiot I am when it comes to cars.

I get asked about my car a lot, which would be great if I knew enough about it.

She wants to get one herself and points at her car. I have no idea what make or model it is. Cars all look the same to me. Four wheels. Windows. The only difference is the color of them.

Her car is blue. Maybe black. It's a dark color. Even naming the color I fail.

I want to ask her about her job, about funny customer stories, about anything for this book, but she's ramping up to go inside and get back to work or start work.

When she goes inside with a smile, I realize the one real shot I had to talk to an employee has gotten away from me. On the last day of the Dunkin tour.

Head hung low, I go in.

It's Halloween. Mid-eighties outside. Not really Fall weather yet. The clocks will fall back this weekend. Florida is supposed to get an arctic blast for a couple of days and drive us into the seventies. Brr.

The woman who hands me my drink offers me Halloween candy on the counter. I spy Whoppers and a KitKat but I'm trying to be good. Besides, I have my pumpkin donut to eat.

I figure a pumpkin donut is fitting today.

Even if it's not Halloween weather.

I grew up in New Jersey, where Halloween was around the time mom started insisting we had to wear jackets and hats if we stepped outside. There was nothing worse than putting on the greatest costume ever and having it covered by a lame jacket, or not being able to wear a cool mask because you had to wear a knitted cap.

You'd walk up to a door and knock, yell trick or treat, and the person with all the power (all the candy) had no idea who you were supposed to be, or if you were even in costume.

Looking back, I'm sure it mattered way more to me than my parents or the lady at the door who wanted to get back to her soap opera.

I'm sitting here trying to remember some of the costumes and can't think of more than one or two, and some of them I might've wanted to wear but never did. I know as I got older I went as the Heavy Metal Dude, sporting my cool mullet (my wife will argue with me on that point) and wearing a Van Halen or Judas Priest concert t-shirt with faded blue jeans, a bandanna for a belt and did I mention the cool mullet?

Other than that "costume" worn for about three straight years until I was deemed too old to walk around town and get free candy, I can't really remember what else I went as. I'm confident my mother went to great lengths to make sure my brother and I looked decent in anything we wore, and I'm sure if she reads this she'll list most of the costumes off the top of her head.

I'm getting old.

I sit and listen to a young guy, maybe in his early twenties, wearing a suit, doing a job interview with a woman who might be interested in the job. She's asking a lot of questions and I'm trying to hear his answers. He seems to know what he's talking about, and when he mentions the salary and benefits I am impressed.

She seems to be impressed, too. She asks him to repeat it, which is funny to me.

No idea what the job actually is. It could be some crazy scam where you have to sell candles or perfume to friends and family. It might be a legit job and this woman will be very happy.

It's fun getting a snapshot of two converging lives. I wonder if she'll be hired or someone else he interviewed will get the position.

I had no idea so many interviews for jobs were being done at a Dunkin, either. It's at least the second I've talked about this month but I've stumbled upon a couple more in the month.

On the other side of this Dunkin a woman is talking loudly on her bluetooth and typing on her laptop conducting business. This might be her office. Maybe she's been here every day, or decided today was the day to get out of the actual office or her house and get some work done.

I will definitely be back to a few of these locations in the future to do some work as well. A good cup of coffee and a donut will get me motivated to write. If nothing else... coffee and a donut.

You don't realize what a hub a Dunkin can be in a community. People come to do work, conduct interviews, make big deals, all while eating and drinking.

If I ever have to get a real job again (fingers crossed it never, ever happens) my goal will be to have a job I'm initially interviewed in a Dunkin. Maybe a job I can work out of the office once a week, and head to Dunkin with my Bluetooth.

The goal is to keep doing this job, which is the best in the world. Living my dream of writing full-time and able to afford to sit in a Dunkin each day for a month and enjoy coffee, donuts and sandwiches.

But all things must come to an end.

As I pack up and leave, I hesitate. This is it.

My month has come to a sudden and quick finale.

It isn't like I'll never be in any of these locations again. In fact, I'll likely venture to most of them in the next year or so. But it will be different.

I know I'll need a few days to process everything. Maybe longer.

This is the end of my month of Dunkin.

Except I have five free beverages I need to get before November ends, so... I'll probably see you tomorrow, seated with my tablet and a large hot coffee Britney Spears within reach.

And the pressure of having to order something different will be over, too.

Yep... living the dream.

Beyond The Month

So... what did I learn?

I learned I like coffee and sandwiches and donuts... not a big surprise there.

I also learned a little bit about myself. While I won't be dramatic and say this was a life-changing exercise, I will admit to having learned a few things.

Notably, I am a creature of habit, and it takes something as drastic as me having to leave the house every day and trying new things, to confront it.

I might be in my fifties (super early fifties, so relax) but at times I feel like the scared little ten year old I used to be, afraid of his own shadow. I was an emotional kid growing up, and I took everything to heart. Reading and music were two focal points I used to get through life. Not that I had it bad at all. In fact, I had an amazing and stable environment, but the problem was inside of me.

An introvert. Unwilling to take risks. Quiet. Geeky. A definite nerd.

Months like this allow me to step away from that person, or the person I used to be, and expand my life without worries.

It also helped me to remember how much a simple ride with the windows down and the music blasting is great for me. I can forget about writing deadlines, problems, anything and everything. I need to remind myself to grab my keys and head off in a random direction once every couple of weeks... and look for a new Dunkin I've never been to.

One bonus to this fun month was meeting new people, eavesdropping on conversations, and having a new cast of future characters for my fiction books. I might've already added some of the conversations and observations just read already in some of my latest stories, too.

Ahh, the life of a writer.

Hopefully, when the book is released, I can revisit some of these spots and get to see some of the many characters I spoke with. Catch up, get their updated stories and drink some coffee.

No matter what, I've bonded with these thirty-plus locations and I'll never look at them the same way. I've even made it a point to go inside instead of just using the drive thru whenever possible.

Some might think my journey wasn't as exciting because I didn't scale a mountain or discover a new life form or deliver a baby kangaroo (random, I know) but to me... it was an epic quest, one that I took physically and mentally.

And got to fill my stomach with deliciousness.

While I wasn't able to do interviews with any of the staff, I think, looking back, it was beside the point. This journey was supposed to be about me bringing in new people and getting their stories and their unique takes.

In the end, I learned a lot about myself and what makes me tick. I also got to share some of the stories about my life most people around me have heard a hundred times. Now the reader gets to hear them.

I am, after all, an old man. Ergo, I get to tell my stories over and over.

Back in my day...

I found a couple of new favorites, too. I am telling you, if you do not immediately go out and get one of their apple fritters, you are making a monumental mistake. Trust me.

You'll also be happy to know I did use all of the free beverages in November. While I didn't leave the house every day, I did manage to get out there and even write in a couple of spots. Some edits and filling in for this book, in fact.

It was inspiring to get to go back to a couple of locations and keep writing.

My goal will be to take a day or two a month and hit a random Dunkin and get some writing in, too.

I also learned something else when it was getting closer to the end of the year, and something I look forward to each year: my Dunkin stats when I use my DD Perks card. Which I always do.

In 2019 I racked up 5,836 points to my Dunkin Perks account.

Had 29 free beverages.

Went to a Dunkin 96 days in the year.

Yes, I am truly a fan. When you take into account I'm in Florida and there isn't a Dunkin on every street corner like in the Northeast, I think I did pretty darn good. I visited a Dunkin better than once every four days. Even factoring out my October, it was still an average of a visit less than every six days. About every week, despite me not wanting to leave the house, I prioritize it for a cup of great coffee and/or a donut.

A long-time reader asked if I would ever do it again, maybe a sequel, or try out another chain. I can tell you two things:

I would love to do this again in Dunkin, but probably won't write a book about it. I'd write a lot of words for books while in Dunkin, which would make me happy. And I have no plans to visit another chain and do the same thing. I'm a loyal Dunkin fan and I'm not really passionate about any other restaurants out there.

My love and loyalty are with Dunkin.

I hope you enjoyed my quirky journey. I know I did. My stomach definitely did.

Now I am off to finish writing a multitude of books and actually leave the house today.

I'm in the mood for a large hot Britney Spears.

Everything I Sampled

Quite simply, every item I ate or drank during October 2019. Obviously, I missed a few combinations and items, but overall I think I had enough variety I could do this another month if I had to.

As if eating at Dunkin every day was something I'd need to be forced to do. Come on. Who am I kidding?

Food (non-donut)

Apple fritter (Day 13)
Bacon, egg and cheese on cinnamon raisin bagel (Day 11)
Big N Toasted (Day 4)
Chicken bacon croissant (Day 6)
Chocolate chip muffin (Day 14)
Cinnamon raisin bagel with cream cheese (Day 1)

Everything bagel with cream cheese (Day 28)
Ham, egg and cheese on English muffin (Day 3)
Fire Roasted Veggie Bowl (Day 5)
Maple bacon sugar sandwich (Day 8)
Plain bagel with cream cheese (Day 12)
Plain bagel with strawberry cream cheese (Day 25)
Power breakfast sandwich (Day 29)
Pumpkin muffin (Day 24)
Sausage egg wrap (Day 26)
Sausage, egg and cheese croissant (Day 27)
Sesame bagel with cream cheese (Day 13)

Drink

Medium hot coffee with cream and sugar (Day 27)
Medium hot coffee, light and sweet (Britney Spears) (Day 5)
Medium hot coffee with almond milk (Day 19)
Medium hot chocolate with caramel swirl (Day 28)
Medium sweet tea (Day 23)
Large cold brew Britney Spears (Day 31)
Large cold brew coffee with caramel swirl (Day 22)
Large cold brew coffee with cream and sugar (Day 4)
Large cold brew coffee with mocha (Day 9)
large dark roast iced coffee with cream and sugar (Day 13)
Large frozen coffee (with whipped cream) (Day 12)

Large hot black coffee (Day 23)

Large hot chocolate (Day 8)

Large hot chocolate with caramel swirl (Day 28)

Large hot coffee with cream, sugar and French vanilla (Day 30)

Large hot coffee with cream and sugar and hazelnut (Day 20)

Large hot chocolate with mint (Day 18)

Large hot coffee, light and sweet (Britney Spears) (Day 2)

Large hot dark roast coffee (Day 25)

Large hot green tea with sugar (Day 16)

Large hot Signature Latte caramel craze (Day 10)

Large hot Signature Latte hot cocoa mocha (Day 6)

Large Ice ChocAuLait (Day 3)

Large iced coffee with cream and sugar (Day 1)

Large iced coffee with cream, sugar and coconut (Day 29)

Large iced macchiato (Day 7)

Large iced Signature Latte with caramel (Day 21)

Large iced Signature Latte with Cinnamon Pumpkin Spice (Day 3)

Large iced Signature Latte with cocoa mocha (Day 14)

Large strawberry coolatta (Day 17)

Large sweet tea with lemon wedges (Day 15)

Large vanilla chai coolatta with whipped cream (Day 14)

Small hot coffee, Britney Spears (Day 11)

Small hot coffee, cream and sugar (Day 12)

Donuts

Apple spice (Day 22)
Chocolate creme filled (Day 17)
Chocolate frosted with sprinkles (Day 19)
Chocolate glazed (Day 2)
Chocolate Munchkins (Day 30)
Double chocolate (Day 19)
Frankenstein monster creme filled (Day 30)
French cruller (Day 19)
Glazed donut (Day 12)
Jelly (Day 23)
Pumpkin (Day 31)
strawberry frosted (Day 17)

Armand Rosamilia is a New Jersey boy living it up in Florida for the past twenty years. He still misses the food, though.

You can follow Armand at his website, where he posts a lot of articles on writing, upcoming releases, random stuff and more!

https://armandrosamilia.com

He would love for you to check out his Fan Club on Facebook, where he posts various things

Armand Rosamilia's Fan Club

He also has a Twitch channel (like one of the cool kids), where he writes live, in real time, with all the umms and ahhs as he tries to stay focused. Riveting to watch!

https://www.twitch.tv/armandrosamilia

Also, feel free to join his Mailing List, where he posts monthly about new releases before anyone else sees them, upcoming deals, rum recipes and more!

He also likes talking in third person, too.